A
BOOK OF
QUIET PRAYER

— peace and prayers —

[signature]

5/22/06

A
BOOK OF
QUIET PRAYER

For All the Seasons, Stages, Moods, and Circumstances of Life

William J. Byron, SJ

Paulist Press
New York/Mahwah, N.J.

Cover design by Sharyn Banks
Book design by Lynn Else

Library of Congress Cataloging-in-Publication Data

Byron, William J., 1927-
    A book of quiet prayer : for all the seasons, stages, moods, and circumstances of life / William J. Byron.
        p. cm.
    ISBN 0-8091-4362-3 (alk. paper)
    1. Prayer—Christianity. I. Title.
    BV210.3.B97 2006
    242'.8—dc22

                                                    2005025491

Published by Paulist Press
997 Macarthur Boulevard
Mahwah, New Jersey, 07430

www.paulistpress.com

Printed and bound in the
United States of America

Contents

❧ ❧

Dedicated to the memory of my mother
Polly Langton Byron
who was the first to introduce me to
the words and ways of prayer

ᔈ ᔇ

Stay quiet with God.
Do not spend your time in useless chatter.
—St. Charles Borromeo

Introduction

❧ ❧

Presumptuous. That's what it is.

Understandably, your initial reaction to the proposition that any author or publisher can tell you what to say in prayer is the dismissive one-word verdict *presumptuous*. Not *ridiculous*, because we all know we could use some help in approaching God, but more than a bit presumptuous to think that one might be capable of putting the guidelines into print. I attempt just that in this book by suggesting ways and words for turning to God in faith, hope, and love, in all stages of life, in all imaginable circumstances: prayer for any time at all. And I do it in a way that may well encourage readers to personalize the prayer and compose a few for themselves, as the Spirit moves. Don't blame me if you can't find an appropriate prayer in these pages; just go ahead and compose your own.

This is a book about praying—special, sometimes privileged conversations and communications with God. "Let us pray" is the familiar, within the walls phrase that invites the gathered faithful to lift their hearts to God and pray aloud together. "Let yourself pray" is what I'm suggesting here; this is an invitation to you on your own terms and timetable to let

1

God touch your life wherever you happen to be, in whatever age, stage, mood, or circumstance you find yourself.

The entire Christian world knows that when Jesus taught his followers how to pray, he did not tell them to say, "My Father." Rather, he instructed them to say, "Our Father" and gave them the other famous words that make up what is known worldwide as the Lord's Prayer. I want to make the point here at the outset that a book like this can, if the reader is not careful, encourage a person to come to prayer with a preoccupation on the "my," the self, and a forgetfulness of the "our" dimension of the approach to God.

"I" have troubles and needs that drive me to pray, but so do "we"—worldwide troubles and needs. To try to go to God without any concern for the needs, joys, fears, hopes, and happiness of others is to display a solipsistic self-centeredness that is unworthy of both the one who prays and the God to whom one lifts his or her mind and heart in prayer. Nothing at all wrong with praying alone, in private and solitude; the mistake is to think you can or should detach yourself from the rest of the human race in order to be in solitude and alone in prayer. Before God, each one of us is all of us.

There will be another book of "quiet prayer" coming along after this one; that book will emphasize praying for and with others, as well as praying for needs that stretch far beyond the boundaries of self. But this small volume encourages you just to look at yourself and God through the narrower windows of your moods, the circumstances in which you find yourself, the seasons, stages, and ages of your life.

How can anyone know what you want to say to God? No one can. I certainly don't pretend to know. I do, however, think I can map out a range of possible paths to be taken by any searching, restless person of faith, who wants consciously to connect with God in prayer. And I think that what you do here will both encourage and enable you to come up with prayers of your own.

That last sentence embodies a few presuppositions of my own that should, at the outset, be made explicit, and will, I'm presuming, be shared by you:

- God is.
- God can be known by faith.
- Faith is a gift.
- The recipient of the gift of faith—the believer—can be nothing but grateful.
- Gratitude is the infrastructure of prayer.
- Prayer—at least the prayer I'm concerned with in this book—is the flame that rises occasionally and consciously from the bed of embers that is one's faith.

Prayer—however, whatever, whenever you communicate with God—requires you to name your God. How do *you* address God? The list of possible names is long; the choice is yours: God, Lord, Abba, Father, Mother, Great One, Holy One, Master, Spirit, Teacher, Creator, Savior, Judge, Redeemer, Friend, My Hope, My Love, My Rock.

I prefer "Lord" (in Latin *Dominus*), even though it might for some connote domination—"lording it over" another—or some other unhelpful emphasis or accent. As I indicated, it is up to the reader to name his or her God with a useful, reverent appellation that says something more, when one sets out to pray, than, "to whom it may concern." Where I say "Lord" anywhere in this book, you insert whatever works best for you.

As a Christian, I, more often than not, pray "through Christ our Lord," because I believe Christ to be divine, the second person of the Blessed Trinity. As an author writing for a general audience, I tend not to make explicit reference in this book to Jesus Christ, although many readers will naturally and reverently see the "Lord Jesus," where the word "Lord" appears in these pages. As the Christian Gospel of John puts it when the apostle Philip asks Jesus to "show us the Father," Jesus says, "Philip, whoever sees me sees the Father" (John 14:7), but that approach to God may not and, almost certainly, will not be a congenial one for the non-Christian, who will nevertheless find relevance in these prayers.

As a Christian, I also find intercessory prayer natural, comfortable, and comforting—asking, for example, Mary, the mother of Jesus, to pray for me. I, and most other Christians I know, pray to the saints in the sense of asking the saints to pray for me. There are patron saints (the one after whom the person was named), model saints (the saint who had a profession or occupation similar to the one now followed on earth by the person who turns to prayer), and so it goes. Saint Jude, patron of lost causes or hopeless cases, gets a lot of business. Other favorites are St. Anthony, the heavenly sleuth who specializes in the retrieval of lost articles ("St. Anthony, St. Anthony, please come around; something's been lost that has to be found!") and Mary's mother, St. Ann, wife of St. Joachim ("St. Ann, St. Ann, get me a man"). The Little Flower—St. Thérèse of Lisieux—died at the age of twenty-four and promised to spend her heaven "doing good upon earth." Many have taken her up on that promise.

St. Joseph, St. Patrick, and St. Peter appear to be most often recruited to be patron saints of Roman Catholic parishes; Saints Dunstan, Alban, and Aiden seem to have a lock on Episcopalian real estate.

Your guardian angel has intercessory power (directed more to assuring your eternal salvation than your rescue from the physical consequences of reckless behavior here on earth).

When dear ones depart, "go home to God," as we sometimes say, our faith tells us that they come into possession of intercessory powers that can be exercised before the throne of God. All you have to do is ask. But neither the angels or saints, nor anyone dear to you who happens to be in heaven, should be regarded by you as labor-saving intermediaries. Listen carefully to this prayer of St. Thomas More: "The things, good Lord, that we pray for, give us the grace to labor for."

The prayer of asking—prayer of petition, as it is often described—is not the sum and substance, beginning and end, be-all and end-all, of prayer. Not by any means. This is not to say that your prayer of petition is unimportant. It is simply to acknowledge that more advanced forms of prayer, contemplative prayer, for example, and other privileged ways of experiencing God, are available to us poor mortals.

Indeed the Holy Spirit wants to pray *within* us, if only we say yes. Nonetheless, the prayer of petition is familiar and just about universal ("Give us this day our daily bread...").

"Gimme, gimme, gimme" is an immature and unsophisticated (even impolite) approach to anyone, let alone to God, your Creator and Lord. Still, God wants to hear from you. Sure, he knows your needs before you articulate them. But in a wonderfully loving and mysterious way, God wants you to enlarge your capacity to receive more and more of his love by stretching out—enlarging—your need-filled soul through your prayers of petition. Ask, and you shall indeed receive. All too often, however, the prayer of petition is misunderstood and misapplied by the one who makes it.

Reflect for a moment on your own personal experience on a lake, a bay, or a river when you are in a boat drawing near to dock. Typically, you would throw a rope (a "line") toward the dock hoping to catch it on a permanent cleat. Once the line is caught on the cleat, you begin to pull. Notice that you are pulling yourself and your boat toward the dock, not the other way around. And yet how often do you toss your prayers of petition up to God, like lines going toward a dock, and immediately try to pull the dock (God) to you! You pray, in effect, for God's will to align itself with yours, for God to come to you, on your terms and conditions, when it should be exactly the other way around.

So, when you pray your prayer of petition—to get that job, make that sale, pass that exam, overcome that cancer— what you must do first is make yourself disposable and disponible to the will of a God who loves you more than you can imagine. Ask for whatever you want, but try to bring yourself to say that you want it only if God wants it for you.

Does God will that you suffer humiliation, pain, suffering? God wills only your ultimate good. God wants to give you love in all circumstances. God may *permit* your suffering, even your victimization, but that is the permissive will (not the direct, positive will) of an all-powerful God at work in the affairs of a world inhabited by human beings whom God gifted with freedom, including the freedom to use their freedom badly—to cheat, harm, maim, murder one another, even innocent others like you. Moreover, you inhabit a world that, due to original sin, the sin of your first parents Adam and Eve, has an unfriendly environment of illness, disease, and death not originally intended by God for those who love him. The original plan did not include cancer, coronaries, hatred, greed, earthquakes, hurricanes, toothaches, kidney stones, or poison ivy. These harsh realities are part of our wounded world (wounded by sin), a world that in its fallen parts is of our own making, a wounded world that shelters and supports as best it can our fallen human nature. So it makes a lot of sense to pray!

Pray for protection from all harm to yourself and others. Pray for safety. Pray for success, prosperity, good health, long life. But condition your prayers of petition with a "your will, not my will, be done."

What's the use of praying if you can't pull God, your dock, toward you? Because God hears you, wants to give you some things *only on condition that you ask,* and in his own mysterious way prescribes *the exercise of asking* as the means of enlarging your capacity to receive the good things he has in store for you.

You pray to a God of mystery, a personal God, an approachable God, but a mysterious God nonetheless. Therefore, you have to bow your head and trust. God is not altogether unknowable, just not fully knowable, and never fully known this side of heaven. Only God knows God completely. So be humble; surely don't act as if you were in fact a "know-it-all" when you pray. Line yourself up with C. S. Lewis who said it so well: "He whom I bow to only knows to whom I bow." Only God (and those to whom God chooses to reveal himself) knows God. And so you bow. And pray!

You exercise your faith when you pray. You may have been misled by your own childhood chant, "Seeing is believing; seeing is believing!" Not true. You have sense knowledge—sensible, perhaps tangible, knowledge of what you see. Faith is not necessary in the presence of sensible, tangible evidence. When you believe, not because you see, but on evidence of the unseen God's promise to be present to you always, ever faithful to you, you "see" with the eye of faith. Believing is seeing with the eye of faith.

In his 1973 book *Images of Faith,* William F. Lynch, SJ, described the "sequence of faith" with just enough of a syntactical jolt to provide a fresh perspective on this age-old reality. Faith "does not see; it hears [the word of God or man], then it inserts this paradigm of hearing into its seeing; its imagining; its experiencing the world." In sum, "Faith does not see; it hears from another."

Let me now ask, as your parents or teachers might have asked years ago: Do you see? Do you get it? Have you got it? Maybe not fully, but you are nonetheless, and in your own way, a believer.

It is as a believer that you come to prayer. Doubt does not disqualify you from the community of believers. Indeed, prayer for the healing of your doubts and unbelief is very good prayer. In the darkness, in the absence of clarity, in the midst of ambiguity, you can bring yourself to prayer, you can permit yourself to say with confidence (confide means "with faith"), "Lord, that I may see!"

CHAPTER ONE

Through the Years

In our more reflective moments we find the reels of memory running back through the years. Imagination can propel us into an unknown future—into those years we hope will come—but it is, more often than not, a rearview mirror that engages the attention of our reflective moments. Mind and memory run back and forth through the years, scanning and surveying, hoping and dreaming, savoring or trying to forget, saying thanks and expressing regrets—the backward glance brings it all to life.

Without realizing it, many people are praying in these reflective moments. Conditioned to think of prayer as activity reserved for sacred space, bent knees, and folded hands, they fail to realize that an always-present, always-interested, ever-loving God is the author of all those years. It is all one moment in God's great view, a moment to be shared again with you in prayer.

You, my reader friend, may not want to begin right here at the beginning of this book. You may find it more congenial to move ahead a few chapters and look for words about forgiveness or failure, or joyful gratitude. This book doesn't have to be read page after page, chapter by chapter.

Let it be a random access companion to your moods, a prompter when you want to reach out to God but are stuck for the right words to use in making contact.

If you are at all inclined at this juncture to look back over the years, to think gratefully or with regret about what has happened through the years, then you may want to pause for a moment and see if you can get a dial tone for a conversation that might begin along these lines…

Looking Back

As far back as I can remember, Lord, you've been there for me. My earliest imaginings of you were in Santa Claus dimensions of generosity—white beard, hearty laugh, warm embrace—and in human reassurance that made me feel safe in darkness and hopeful in light. Now I think of you more as Power and Presence distinct from me, but also somehow mysteriously beside me, even within me.

I'm not good at retrieving earliest memories, Lord; I just like to think of you as being there for me, being there without my calling on you, being there to be counted on by me whenever I paused to think about it.

Those pauses were infrequent, I admit. I was so busy discovering life and figuring out the riddle of myself. But you were always there for me.

From my present vantage point that stretches back through the years, I can see more clearly now that you touched me through the love of others, and I saw you in the faces of love that surrounded me. For all of that, all I can say is thanks.

Go right on, on your own, saying thanks in any way you wish for whatever comes to mind. But perhaps, my reader friend, that is not the way it is, or was, with you. You may perhaps not be able to find all that much to be thankful for, as you look back. You may be decidedly uncomfortable in the presence of the Lord (whom you may have been conditioned to think of as big cop, or unsmiling umpire, or tough warden, instead of a source of goodness and love). Maybe "Father" is all it takes to make you want to forget all about those early years. You may be more inclined to say...

Here I am, Lord, and I'm really not sure why. I'm not sure why I'm attempting to pray at the moment. I'm not even sure I know why I exist, why I am—anywhere at anytime. Existence is a mystery to me—mine as well as yours. If you are my all-loving, all-powerful Father, I have to wonder about my participation in the gene pool! I'm not the loving person I'd like to be; I'm anything but powerful in my engagements with life.

Maybe I think about this stuff too much. Or, maybe I don't think about it nearly as often as I should. If I thought more often of my origins, a certain sense of wonder might slip into my consciousness. I'm not easily awed, but a bit of awe might begin to dawn when I think of the dimensions of creation and—what else can I call it?—the wonder of it all. It might be useful, even helpful, for me to force myself, in your presence, to think about the wonder of me!

I have to admit that there have been many good influences on me through the years. There have been many roads not taken, however, and many opportunities passed up. Help me, Lord, to focus on the positives, not the negatives, and let that focus fix my mind on you—at least for awhile. That will surely be enough for now.

"Looking back" will put you in touch with places and faces, architectural and human milestones, or signposts that have been there for you along the way. Some of those images will make you want to pick up your pace in putting distance between yourself and the past. Others will make you want to return in an *Our Town* kind of way to enjoy the company of old friends, to experience the warmth of family love, to know once again the security of neighborhoods and playing fields and familiar landmarks.

It is more than possible that you can experience God in these memories. If you acknowledge God to be indeed your Creator, your Origin and ultimate Destiny, a "return-to-sender" exercise like this can be not only prayer but fun for those who take the time. Taking time is essential for growth in prayer. A priest friend of mine who made an extended "retreat" each year—eight days of solitude away from work, the news, phones, and friends—used to say you have to be willing to "waste time with the Lord in prayer," if you want to make progress as a truly human being. But any genuinely prayerful retreat is not an escape; it is a prayerful pause in order to gain clearer vision for...

Looking Ahead

Looking ahead points you, by definition, toward the future. That may be a direction you are not anxious to consider at the moment. You may be like most other members of the human race who prefer to live in the immediate past. Even if you are adventuresome and courageous in the face of the unknown, you may still be a bit hesitant about stepping up, out, and into new and unfamiliar surroundings. But you can't steer a parked car. You've got to get yourself rolling.

Looking ahead invites you to hope, to be hopeful, a perspective that will get some attention later in this book in chapter 5. For the moment, I will be content to credit G. K. Chesterton with the idea and put his thought into my own words: "Hope is really no virtue at all unless things are really hopeless!"

Think about that. Making a virtue of hope means putting your hope in something or someone (and thus drawing strength to move ahead). Who better to hope in than God? That's why hope, along with faith and love, is called a theological virtue—its object is God.

Unbelievers have hope, as some will say, "in the future," and they take comfort in that connection. But with what do they think they are connecting? Novelist Douglas Coupland has a character in *All Families Are Psychotic* (Bloomsbury, 2001) say, "I stopped believing in the future— which is to say, I stopped thinking of the future as being a place, like Paris or Australia—a place you can go *to*. I started to believe that we're all going, going, going all the time, but there's no city or place at the end. We're just going, that's all." The "future," no matter how you view it, is no substitute for the destination the believer calls God!

Similarly, you will often be advised to "follow your dreams" and the direction of those dreams is always forward. But is anything that resembles reality the point of departure or the expected destination of your dreams? You should indeed be a dreamer, a hope-filled, faith-based dreamer. The Lord, speaking through the prophet Joel (2:28–29), said: "Then afterward I will pour out my spirit upon all flesh; your sons and your daughters shall prophesy, your old men shall dream dreams, and your young men shall see visions. Even on the male and female slaves, in those days, I will pour out my spirit."

Spirit-filled dreams and visions for a better future for both young and old. What a thrilling prospect! Surely something to pray on, pray for, and pray about.

Lord, let me see the future through the eye of my heart.
Lift my heart to see ahead,
> *and let my single-heartedness—grounded in you—stay*
> > *the course.*
Over land, over sea,
> *through the tunnels of discouragement,*
> *through this setback, or that reversal;*
> *on the heights, in the depths,*
> *on the bricks, in the pits,*
> *wherever I happen to be on the growing edge of life,*
> *keep me pointed, Lord, toward a future full of hope.*
I know this means that I will be pointed toward you.
I also know it means that you are always pointed (not
> *pointing at, but positioned)*
> > *toward me.*
Someone once said that

"a poor man is not a man without a dime;
he's a man without a dream."
No matter how many dimes I may or may not have on any
given day, Lord,
I pray for Spirit-driven dreams that keep me moving
ahead—toward you.

Decades

I was well along into adulthood when I decided to pro-
nounce this word "deck-aides" instead of "deck-edds," as I
had most often heard it pronounced. It has a stronger ring to
it—decADES—and that stronger sound suggests to me a set
of building blocks, one on top of the other. How the decades
do add up, pile up, stack up, without your even noticing! But
(to let the imagination run for a moment), like it or not, your
head and face are there at the top of the stack.

Things don't look all that much different from your
perspective. But you look a bit different to others, particu-
larly to others who haven't seen you for quite awhile.
Schools and colleges are trying to be helpful at reunion time
when they give you a name tag with your yearbook picture
attached—helpful to others, maybe, but a bit of a jolt for
you. Now you know how movie stars feel when they happen
to see reruns of their films made decades ago!

What can be delightfully and unexpectedly helpful to
you as the decades add up is the spectacle of an older person
smiling. Those smiles seem to say, as the words of Robert
Browning, engraved on a sundial I once saw, put it: "Grow
old along with me! The best is yet to be...." And the words

of Browning that complete this thought are:... "the last of life for which the first was made!" Even though they experience the "edge of sadness" associated with the sunset years, smiling elders convincingly communicate, by their smiles, that something wonderful lies ahead.

Those who belong to what Tom Brokaw labeled *The Greatest Generation* can examine with a mixture of love, pride, and sorrow a set of blocks that have their foundation in the Great Depression and then progress through high school years, World War II, college or special training for beneficiaries of the GI Bill, new jobs, new cars, and television in the 1950s. Marriage and other commitments fit in here as well. And then came the turmoil of the 1960s, and then you'll find a mixture of memories encapsulated in the blocks of the 1970s, 1980s, 1990s, on into this present century. As with building blocks at any age, your decades can be arranged to match your personal chronology and the memories you've collected through the years. You might then be inclined to pray:

Lord, my decades are your gift to me,
And I regret that I haven't always thought of them as gifts.
They are packaged now not so neatly on the shelf of
*   memory.*
It would be ungracious of me not to give you thanks,
*   and praise as well, for decades past and decades yet to*
*   come.*
And so I say, thank you, Lord.
Memories are always of the past.
Let me pause now in your presence to savor those
*   memories....*

Making memories is one way I can think about what I'm
doing in the present.
No one can say with certainty that a given number of
decades remain
to be experienced and enjoyed.
I can't be bothered worrying about that.
I simply ask that you shore up with your grace the decades
beneath my feet
and thus provide me with a secure foundation for
welcoming whatever lies ahead.

Years

The psalmist had a way with words, sometimes pointed, more often gently reassuring, but always to the point: "...our years come to an end like a sigh. The days of our life are seventy years, or perhaps eighty, if we are strong; even then their span is only toil and trouble; they are soon gone, and we fly away" (Ps 90:9–10).

Everyone, except the young, knows that we have very few years to be young. Some of us experience moments that seem to be as big as a year (and they are not always painful!), but they cannot be properly appreciated except within the framework of the years. We tend, most of us, to take our years 365 days at a time, and growing numbers of us would point a modern-day psalmist toward updated actuarial tables that show a lengthier life span than might have been reasonably expected when the psalms were sung in ancient Israel.

You may have heard about the fellow who became an actuary because he couldn't stand the excitement of accounting. Exciting or not, someone has to count both beans and years to let us know where we stand, where we begin, and where we leave off. And no matter how loosely or carefully the count is done, no one seriously expects an unlimited allotment of years on this planet. But we don't like to talk about that. No one but the psalmist, that is.

So we should be wise enough to listen and sensible enough to think through the implications of a finite (and relatively brief) span of years. Why not talk that over with the Lord?

Lord, I'm no linguist, but I suspect year and yore have
much in common.
I didn't think much of years as discrete measures of time
when I was young;
I thought of them as measures of superiority—"I'm ten;
I'm older than you!"
I'm now older maybe (and trying to hide it),but not much
wiser.
If I had been wise I would have taken care then to begin
unpacking my years—
those just ended or about to begin—
and review what was done in the past or might be
done in the future with each of its 365
precious parts.
The days of yore—the good old days or bad old days of
yore, were packaged in years I actually lived.
The days to come will be packaged into years. I can, with a
bit of planning,
arrange my days to fill my years, but I now have
enough sense, I think, not to attempt
doing that on my own.
Lord, I need your help.

*Help me to choose wisely, not just to collect the days
ahead.*
*Help me to live gently, not walking thoughtlessly over the
moments that are mine.*
*Help me to appreciate the trust you place in me when you
give me another year.*
And grant me the grace to be faithful to that trust. Amen.

My reader friend, I invite you to make what sense you
can of the meaning William Butler Yeats intended when he
wrote the following lines: "The years like great black oxen
tread the world./ And God the herdsman goads them on
behind,/ And I am broken by their passing feet" (*The
Countess Cathleen*, Act IV). You are not yet broken and
need never be. If indeed the years can be thought of as coming at you from behind, don't look back; just keep moving
ahead. Try running, even if you think the "passing feet" of
the years are at your back and ready to break you.

Recall the joke about the two hikers who encountered a
great black bear on a mountain trail. The bear growled and
moved toward them; they started to run. "Why are we running?" one asked the other, "he's faster than both of us." "I'm
running," the other replied, "because I'm faster than you!"

The years are out there waiting for you. Like Robert
Frost, you've got miles to go before you sleep. Run, don't
walk, toward the year ahead.

Months

I had a friend who used to say, "I went on a month-long diet,
and all I lost was thirty days!" When you're dieting, a month

can be a very long time. When you're on vacation, a month can evaporate quickly and easily.

A month is a "measure." The word is related etymologically to "moon," and perhaps as well to *mens,* the Latin word for *mind* (often taken to be the measure of a person). Women are conditioned by nature to understand periodicity, cycles, *menses.* They more easily than men acquire a sense of the rhythms of life and the movement of life, month by month.

Calendar nomenclature is interesting. Why are the "number" months—"seven" for September, "eight" for October, "nine" for November, "ten" *(decimus)* for December—moved forward to positions nine, ten, eleven, and twelve, respectively, on the Gregorian calendar? I'll leave that to you to figure out. Why do the other eight months have the names they have, and the places they occupy on the calendar?

The months put a metronome on the year. They pace us. They measure our progress fairly because they are too long to be called impulse, and too short to qualify as seasons or phases. They are what they are—thirty-day, give-or-take—portions of a human life.

Perhaps you belong to a book-of-the-month club, or you may look forward each year to National Poetry Month, or Black History Month. Or, you may have earned the right where you work to occupy the employee-of-the-month parking space. You're literally surrounded by month markers, once you pause to think about it and begin to count them up.

If taken in thirty-day segments, planning is less intimidating. So is budgeting (and, of course, any budget is a plan).

Might prayer fit into thirty-day patterns? It can in at least two ways: a monthly meeting with a spiritual director, or a month-long period of prayerful reflection in a special retreat setting. These monthly markers are relatively rare, surely not typical, in the prayer practice of most believers. But now that your mind is stretched in a thirty-day framework, try praying within that framework along the following lines:

Lord of all my days, months, and years,
*   even though I know I cannot predict the future,*
I think I can see thirty days ahead.
As happens on a long automobile drive at night,
*   when I have headlight help for only 80 or 90 yards at*
*   a stretch,*
*   but get another 80 or 90 yards of illumination*
*   once the earlier stretch is traversed,*
*   so my one-month prayer perspective can move me*
*   closer to you, bit by bit, day by day.*
In your presence, I take it one day at a time, but I want to
*   lay out a month-long plan.*
Thanks, Lord, for the ideas.
Thanks for the goals.
Thanks for the energy I have to cooperate with your grace
*   and put this all in motion.*
Don't let me just sit idly or walk aimlessly; plant purpose
*   in my heart.*
Keep me focused within the immediacy of this next month,
*   these next thirty days.*
I can see you, Lord, in it all, behind it all, through it all.
May the month ahead be a measure of my need for you,
*   and of my love as well.*

Weeks

I don't know whether kids today still play a card game called "Fifty-two Pickup." Probably not, because they're a lot smarter than we were when we would agree to play that game only to have a plotting playmate throw the full deck—fifty-two cards—on the floor and say, "OK, go ahead and pick 'em up!"

There are, of course, fifty-two weeks in a year. Think of the year—the whole year—as a deck of cards. Your last year may have begun or ended in a "Fifty-two Pickup" mode of confusion and incoherence—mixed-up weeks, shuffled out of any order.

You "shuffle the deck" as your first line of defense in a card game; you "arrange your cards" before deciding on your strategy in "playing your hand." And, of course, you play the hand you've been dealt, as best you can.

I once saw a deck of cards that functioned as a calendar. Each card represented one week of the year. Each suit in the deck represented a season of the year. The designer of this calendar, Julie Mabey, says she likes "to think of a calendar as marking time in a circle or spiral that keeps returning to the same events and traditions that I chose to highlight each year." How true that is. A calendar can mark your habits, keep track of your memories, target your planning on recurring annual events. There is a joker in every deck, of course, so be advised that you can make provision for unexpected happenings that can turn up (or down) in any given week.

You can shuffle your deck of weeks for a game of Solitaire. You'll notice right away how unpredictable patterns emerge. Even though you want to take life day by day, or week by week, you will never be free of surprises and encounters with the unexpected, despite your best intentions to keep things in "proper order." But weeks are made to be managed. Every Monday is there to give you a chance for a fresh start. And so, you might want to pray:

Lord, let me manage my weeks well, especially my next one.
The next seven days will come to me as so many gifts, if I
  choose to see them that way.
I could "roll a seven," I know, but I'm not counting on
  that, at least not yet.
Relying on your help, your sustaining grace,
  I want to take a moment now to lay it out for the
  week ahead.
Who needs my help, Lord?
Where will I find you this week, Lord?
What did I leave undone last week that might deserve some
  attention now?
When will I have a chance to offer words of encouragement,
  praise, and thanks?
Why do I find it so hard to do for others what I always
  want them to do for me?
There's another week waiting for me, Lord.
Let me go out to meet it.
Help me to use it well.

Days

Day by day. That's the rhythm of life for most of us.

St. Augustine, reflecting on what it means "to dwell in the house of the LORD my whole life long" (Ps 23:6), noted, "There, the days do not come and go in succession, and the beginning of one day does not mean the end of another; all days are one, simultaneously and without end, and the life lived out [there] has itself no end." Well, we're not there yet! We meet our days, and make what we can of them, one at a time.

Just keep putting one foot in front of the other and you'll find yourself making it, getting there—day by day. "Take them one day at a time," they've been telling you all these years, and they're right. But they're also presuming that you've laid out something resembling a plan that stretches over the weeks and months, into the years, and on into the future, which, although not a place, is a destination.

Just like that journey of a thousand miles that begins with a single step, so the destiny that is yours begins with the day at hand. Not that your day is your destiny. You are a whole lot freer than that. But yours is a restless freedom, driven by desires and dreams.

There is a Hindu wisdom-saying that gets us closer to the point I'm trying to make: "You are what your deep driving desire is/ As your desire is, so is your will/ As your will is, so is your deed/ As your deed is so is your destiny."

Let your dreams drive your days. Try not to "lose" a day because you might also lose a portion of your dream and thus fall short of your destiny. Have great respect for the everlasting importance of this day—the one you call "today." It is all yours and no one has one with more minutes or hours than the day that is yours today. So why not pray?

So thank you, Lord, for gifting me, and blessing me not
*   least with the gift of this day.*
Lord, thank you for the gift of this day.
Thank you for the gift of myself—my life, my health,
*   my faith, my friends, my loves, my talents—*
*   and for the gift of this very day where all these other*
*   gifts converge.*
Without this day, I would not have a cup to hold these
*   other gifts.*
I would not be able to drink deeply of the joys you share
*   with me, day by day, one day at a time.*
There are seven days in each of my weeks,
*   and seven times seventy reasons for giving thanks on*
*   every one of them.*

Light and Darkness

Light and darkness are the scissors that divide our days one from another and thus prepare them for packaging into weeks, months, and years. Then the years are packaged into decades and a life span is produced—all as a result of the division of light from darkness.

It's been said that John the Evangelist wrote as Rembrandt painted—in shades of light and darkness. Out of the darkness of unbelief, the curious inquirer Nicodemus comes, "by night," to the Light, in John's Gospel (3:1–2).

The darkness of doubt can, by the grace of God, give way to the dawn of faith. "In the beginning was the Word," a reference, of course, to Jesus who was, in John's presentation, "...the light of all people." And this evangelist, this bearer of good news, proclaims that "the light shines in the darkness, and the darkness did not overcome it" (John 1:1, 4–5).

We think of light in at least two ways: illumination and weight. We dismiss a pseudointellectual as a "lightweight." We recall certain boxers as "light-heavyweight" champions and rarely reflect on the possibility of contradiction in that twin-termed title. We all have our "lighthearted" moments.

Illumination in our personal experience is real and figurative. Light bulbs, flashlights, headlights, and spotlights are all quite familiar and often quite necessary. Enlightenment follows an explanation; "bright ideas" come from time to time; we are sometimes privileged to receive "lights" in prayer.

Light lifts our moods. Darkness deepens our doubts and fears. When differences are sharpened in our awareness, we see them clearly, "like night and day." Light and darkness are part of every life; they are woven into the human condition. That's why either end of that spectrum can point us toward prayer.

"I believe; help my unbelief" (Mark 9:24) are words that I
find reassuring,
and so I make them my own as I come out of my
personal darkness
toward you, the everlasting Light.

*I pray, Lord, for light—to know you, my God, to discover
  your will for me,
  and to find the path you want me to follow through
  both light and darkness.
I sometimes think of myself as a five-watt bulb when it
  comes to searching for
  and understanding your plan for me.
Faith persuades me there is a plan ("help thou my
  unbelief"), but the darkness of doubt,
  like the summer fog, sometimes surrounds me.
All I can do is turn toward you, and,
  flitting spiritual moth that I am,
  hope that you, my Light, will draw me to yourself,
  where I will have not only a fleeting glimpse of you,
  but a look, however brief, at your plan for me.
So I fall silent now in your presence, awaiting that glimpse
  and hoping for that look.*

So Swift, So Sad, and Yet...

It all goes by so fast. That's what they're thinking, and sometimes saying, in nursing homes and assisted living centers
where nothing appears to be moving fast, and most of the
action focuses on mealtimes. That, of course, is sad. So swift
the passage of the years, so sad the waiting for the end.

An aging, but not yet aged father, used to amuse his
young adult children by indicating that he knew what they
would be routinely saying to one another in just a few more
years: "I went last week. It's your turn to visit him now. Why
are you always expecting me to be the one who drives out
there to see him?" When he died suddenly at age seventy-

five, they all were there for the funeral. They wept; they miss him still.

So swift, so sad.

Do you "fall and break your hip," as you often hear it said? Or, do you break your hip and fall, as some medical observers suggest? Those bones and muscles, those arms and legs that once were so strong, grow brittle or flaccid with the passage of time. The time that once flew by now lies heavy on the hands. The person who was fleet of foot now doesn't even want to think about having "one foot in the grave."

So swift, so sad.

And yet there is so much more to the story of a human life that runs fully through the years. There is the measureless expanse of eternity waiting to be explored and enjoyed in the love of the eternal God. The "and yet" dimension of our lives introduces a hope-based eagerness to the evening of our lives. Not an eagerness for death, but an expectation, grounded in faith, of eternal happiness. "Lord, I believe, help my unbelief."

I do indeed believe, Lord, in you, in your love for me,
*   in the promises you have given me.*
And I can't believe that you can be
*   anything but faithful to your promises.*
You promised me that I will live forever.
You promised that if I trust you, you will shelter me, save
*   me.*
Your strengths, you have promised, will offset my
*   weaknesses.*
Your wisdom will erase my foolishness.

When there is nothing of me (and it is looking more that
way every day), there will be, you assure me, more of
you.
And when I am no more as I and others have known me to
be, there will be no more sickness or swiftness, no
more sadness, just the "and yet"
of endless joy in eternal life.

I am sad no more because I am with you, and you with
me, forever.

And so it goes, for all of us, through the years, through all
the years—long or short, the good years and the bad—
through all the years that lead us home to God.

CHAPTER TWO

Seasons

Funny, isn't it, the way we use the word *season*. A *seasoned* veteran offers advice that is worth heeding. A bit more *seasoning* will make that dish a genuine delight. *Four Seasons* says *luxury hotel* to those who move in the loftier social circles. But for most of us, *season* means the seasons of the year—autumn, winter, spring, and summer. Most of us have a favorite. Some of us, by geographic circumstance, don't enjoy the fourfold variety of winter snows, springtime blossoms, summer sun, and autumn leaves. All of us, however, are familiar with the seasons of life.

Mary Flynn was a popular professor of social work at the Catholic University of America. First and foremost, she was a wonderful wife and mother. Mary arranged her teaching schedule so that she could be home at lunchtime with and for her children, whose elementary school was just a couple of blocks from their home.

When Mary died, her young adult children held a wake service for her at home. Hundreds of friends passed through the house to offer condolences and express both sympathy and love. A homemade prayer service included vocal remembrances from the then adult children Mary left behind.

One daughter recalled a troubled moment in her twelve-year-old life when she found herself at home at lunchtime with her mother on a bitterly cold winter day as the body of the mother of the child's best friend lay "somewhere" in a casket, as yet unburied, because the frozen ground could not be opened for a grave. "Promise me you won't die in winter," the daughter recalled saying to her mother. "When will you die, Mom, do you know?"

And Mary Flynn, without answering, simply walked over to the phonograph, selected a record from the rack, put it on the turntable, and returned to sit beside her daughter and hug her as they listened to the voice of Robert Goulet singing "If Ever I Would Leave You." The lyrics moved melodically through the four seasons, providing a memorable background for the reassurance a mother's embrace was able to give to an anxious child.

Summer

"Can we make the camp season longer and the school year shorter?" asks a departing camper in mid-August, as he leaves lakeside for city at summer's end.

Everyone has good early memories of summer. Being swept ashore with the surf, floating in an inner tube on a lake, splashing around in the pool, catching lightning bugs, chasing butterflies. Memories recall Fourth of July fireworks, band concerts, baseball games, amusement parks, bike rides, roasted marshmallows, hamburgers and hot dogs, thunder and lightning, reading on the porch, sailing, waterskiing, summer jobs, hiking, fishing, and just hanging out.

We tend to remember more readily what we came up with ourselves as "something to do," rather than the events that were organized for us. But we will always be grateful for those trips and family outings that we, in later life, take pains to provide for our own children and grandchildren.

Some parents inevitably find themselves asking, "Is it worth the hassle?" as they deplete their supply of patience and exhaust their peacemaking skills during long automobile trips that are part of the family vacation. Yes, it's worth it. The happy memories remain with those kids throughout their lives. "D'ya remember when we...?" Yes we certainly do.

Thank you, Lord, for summers past and summers
yet to come.
Thanks for all the fun—fun with a purpose, like those
great days at camp,
and fun for nothing else but the fun of it—
in the attic, the cellar, the playgrounds,
the farms, the meadows, and the woods.
Thanks for summer rest, romance, and reflection.
There were summer moments, Lord, when you came
toward me,
"walking on the waters," in a sense, as I felt your
presence in my life and caught a glimpse of
your plan for me.
I've deviated from the plan, I know,
and I'm grateful for the midcourse corrections that
your providence provided for me from time to time.
Thank you also for the rains of summer, Lord, and
the growth-inducing summer sun
that produced the crops and flowers and all things
fresh.

Thanks for summer nights and summer sounds,
for love songs and for everything that summer
sings to me now
by way of grateful thought and happy memory.

Autumn

Diane Sherwood is the only person I know who could have pulled it off. Forced by cancer to leave her job as associate director of the Washington Interfaith Conference, she underwent treatment at the Washington Hospital Center. When advised that chemotherapy could do no more for her, and that no other treatment would work, she told me with a smile, "I'm going home to die."

I was Diane's pastor. I gave her the sacrament of the sick, the anointing with holy oil accompanied by prayers for her return to health, if God so willed. Or, if it was time for her to leave this world, the anointing was intended to give her strength to bear any loneliness or fear that might touch her during her final days. At home, friends came to pray. Both Diane and they talked about planning her funeral. Then an idea came to her: "Why not a celebration of life before I die? Not my life, but the gift of life and friendship. Let's do it in an interfaith setting." Since the promotion of interreligious understanding was an important part of her life, it was not surprising to hear Diane say, "Something new is breaking open. We're coming together in our day to create new bonds of interfaith friendship; we are finding new ways of partnering."

So, on Labor Day 2002, at 4:00 in the afternoon, several hundred people gathered at Tifereth Israel Synagogue in

Washington, DC, for a Celebration of Life. Diane was there at the center of it all. The prelude was the Gayatri Mantra Chant, a favorite of Diane's. The president of the synagogue welcomed everyone. The Protestant minister who heads the Interfaith Conference explained, as the printed program indicated, "why we are here." Next, music from the Baha'i community, followed by a congregational song led by a guitar-playing rabbi. A female Episcopal priest led a guided Meditation on Life. Then there was a Sikh prayer, with drum and strings, led by a turbaned friend who introduced himself as Diane's dentist. A woman who founded the Martin Luther King Support Group read an excerpt from Dr. King's writings. A Jewish layperson read the Prayer of St. Francis to the rabbi's guitar accompaniment. Then the physician who heads the Neonatal Intensive Care Unit at Georgetown University Hospital shed his shoes and stood at the podium to offer a Hindu prayer. After the "passing of peace," the director of the Mormon Choir of Washington led the group in singing "How Great Thou Art." Diane's sister and two nieces spoke about faith and family. Next, I read Romans 12:1–21. After that Diane spoke to the assembly from her wheelchair and from her heart. And then, to chanting and drumming in the spirit of Eastern religions, the group moved downstairs for a reception and table discussion about their religious similarities and differences.

When it was all over, a Catholic woman, one of about one hundred Catholics in the assembly, said to me, "I've never been so convinced as I am right now that we are all praying to the same God."

As Cardinal Walter Kasper, of Germany, said in his Washington lecture to the Catholic Common Ground Initiative in June 2002, "[I]nterreligious dialogue, especially the dialogue with Judaism, has become a defining characteristic of the life of the Church. In fact, since the Second Vatican Council dialogue has become a fundamental expression and feature of Catholicism." And he added, "As human beings, we do not only carry on dialogue, we are dialogue."

Diane Sherwood gave a smiling "amen" to that in what she suspected (correctly) would be the last September of her life. The book you are holding in your hands, my reader friend, encourages you, as dialogue, to continue your conversation with God through all the seasons of the year.

School bells ring in autumn all across the United States as August yields to September. Falling leaves and flaming foliage come to those parts of the country where climates favor cold snaps, shorter days, and deciduous or leaf-shedding trees. "Fall back and spring forward" is the parental explanation to children wondering about the disappearance of daylight saving time. Springtime now seems so far away. An edge of sadness accompanies an autumnal awareness of the passage of time and the fragility of life.

For some, the distraction of football and marching bands helps the mind disengage itself from the "Hazy, Lazy Days of Summer" and connect with the reality of work—schoolwork or some other segment of workplace reality. Back to normal is a typical adult description of the season we call autumn.

Autumn without sunlight would be unimaginable. Autumn without rain would delay the return of those colder days that have been standing by, waiting for their annual reentry into our lives. Indian Summer, that lovely span of warm afternoons that take us by surprise shortly after the first frost, lifts our spirits briefly before letting us gently down into the vestibule of winter. That, at least, is how I remember the change of seasons from summer to fall.

Fall is another name we give to this time of year. The season gets this name from the falling leaves. *Autumn* works better for those who have no leaves to gather up and bag (where years ago they used to burn), and no colored leaves to trace and mount on construction paper and post on schoolroom walls. *Autumn* as a word may have a root relationship to words in other languages for increase or augment, as the crops increase to their harvest readiness in the season we call autumn. Much more likely, the word simply means autumnal, not autonomous, just autumnal—transitional from warm to cold.

The human heart can find itself growing that way too. That's why the edge of sadness that comes with this season cannot be left to grow beyond the dimensions of a hint or suggestion. Check it at the onset. Brush it off and look ahead with confidence. The best is yet to come.

Lord, I pray to you in the autumn of the year;
*   it might be for me the autumn of life.*
I know what is behind; I have no idea how
*   much time there is to go.*
I'm always in transition; I'm autumnal in so
*   many ways.*
Crisp air reminds me that I'm alive.

Clear skies invite my reach to exceed my grasp,
to reach toward you as toward a goal,
to stretch my soul toward you.
Thanksgiving is a day in every autumn;
it is also a state of mind for anyone as graced
as I've been graced.
Thanks for life, Lord. Thanks for autumn.
And thanks for the sunshine that brings the leaves
and me to full color
long after the greener days are gone.

Winter

The title of John Steinbeck's novel, *The Winter of Our Discontent*, comes spontaneously to my mind with the word *winter*. Why not Shakespeare's *The Winter's Tale*, or why not jingle bells and holiday cheer? I really don't know, but I suspect it has something to do with shortened days, leafless trees, patches of ice underfoot, and gray clouds overhead. Not to mention sniffles and chills.

The normal, abiding restlessness of the human heart gets contained indoors in wintertime, clogged up like crankcase oil or slow to move like honey in a jar. That, at least, is winter for me, even though I can and do enjoy the beauty of snowfall and lawns and fields carpeted with snow under blue skies and a friendly sun.

I've lived a few winters in warmer climes, but even there those January, February, and March days are different. Not blustery and cold, perhaps, but different nonetheless.

Winter is so often humdrum, routine, nose-to-the-grindstone, bundled up, and confining. The mind runs wild but, in the circles where so many of us move, the toes stay cold. There are, of course, wool socks and warm sweaters; logs on the fire and fires in the fireplace; good books and good friends; family laughter and family love; music, wine, casseroles, warm words and warm food. And best of all, especially for those whose memories of winter reach back over many decades, there is the resurrection hope of spring-time, the realization that winter's dead spots will all spring back to life. As will be the case, we prayerfully hope, for all of us.

Thank you, Lord, for the gift of winter.
For the helpful reminder that a death of sorts is a
necessary preamble to life, I say thanks.
For the cold that makes me grateful for human warmth
and nature's heat,
for the gray days that underscore the precious
brightness of the sun,
for the slowdown time to get in touch with
myself and with you,
I say thanks.
Winter is beautiful anywhere in the world,
as long as winter's people
remember their springtime birth, summertime
growth, and autumnal preparation
for wintertime reality.
Help me to remember, Lord, with gratitude.
Help me to move through winter with hope in you.

Spring

It is so easy to smile when you simply say the word *spring*. You find yourself outdoors now and smiling. The hold of winter's grip (and grippe) is broken. You want to walk (maybe even run), and smile; you want to meet and talk; you want to be on the move. It is spring again!

Younger than springtime? Maybe not, but young at heart and smiling. You may have very good reason to be sad, reason that respects no season, but springtime wants you to pack away that sadness with your winter clothes.

Spring fever? There is probably a medical basis for that expression somewhere in pediatric literature, but the implied slowdown has to yield to the ubiquitous evidence of a spring-in-the-step and a smile on the face. If fever it be, let it be an elevated expectancy for better days ahead.

The flowers of spring? That familiar phrase says, or better, sings it all, doesn't it? Weeks earlier there were just buried bulbs and barren branches; now look at the display of life. And you, with that springtime smile, are indeed "as welcome as the flowers of spring" to dear old wherever you call home.

Some think of spring cleaning; others of spring break. Everyone thinks green, not as the color of money, but the color of hope. The greening of the spirit is part of any springtime cleaning up and breaking away. *Wheat That Springeth Green* is not simply the title of a novel; it is also nature's reminder that everything needed to sustain both life and hope is there for you.

Life, as you know it on this beautiful earth, cannot last forever. You acknowledge that with a touch of sadness, perhaps, but with your faith firmly planted and, by virtue of your faith, you stand prepared.

Those in the "eldering" ranks, elder their way with measured steps into another springtime each year. The youngsters, God bless them, take carefree hops, skips, and jumps into their unknown future. Whether you are eldering out or jumping in, or somewhere in between, you have plenty of reason to pray when the greening begins around you and the gratitude wells up from within.

Lord of all creation, Lord of heaven and earth,
    be Lord of all my hopes and dreams.
Protect me from the trap of self-sufficiency and
        preserve me
        from even the hint of a suggestion that I
        can make my own grass grow,
        or bring the trees of my talents to life.
But more than anything I ask you to preserve me
        from despair.
No matter how dark the days, how deep
        the disappointment;
        no matter how humiliating the defeat
        or great the loss,
        you are always there to bring me back to life.
That is springtime for me. That is hope forever green.
That is truth unchangeable, love undying, leading,
        as you alone can lift and lead me
        to everlasting life.

So, there they are: the seasons of life, the seasons in prayer. You've traveled "through the years" in the first chapter of this book; you've enjoyed four seasons of faith-based reflection in the chapter that ends right here. In subsequent chapters you can bring your stages of life and your circumstances *in* life to prayer along with your own familiar moods. And I would certainly encourage you to keep on going, beyond the last page of this book, to pray for your friends, your special needs, and the needs of others. I intend to provide you with a follow-up book, a sequel to this one, that will give you some encouragement and guidance along that worthwhile way.

It is curious, but nonetheless true, that you can stand alone before the one God but, at the same time, you cannot go to God alone. You can stand alone before God at any time in prayer (this book is written to assist you in taking that posture), and you will eventually stand there again alone, before God, in judgment. But you go to God with others, all others who were created and redeemed by an all-powerful, all-loving God; inclusion of those others is the business of the follow-up book.

You were born alone, yes, but to others, without whom you could never have been born. You go through life with others and have a chance to know, love, and serve them on the way. You will die alone, true, but your death will be a separation from one community, a covenant community, and entry into another, a communion of saints. False modesty may lead you to protest that you don't belong in the company of saints, but that's the only company there is on the other side of death for those who love God. Another alter-

native awaits those who love neither God nor neighbor, but
the God you meet in prayer has promised you salvation from
all that.

The Old Testament tells you that your participation in
the saving covenant God made with us is not as an individ-
ual, but as a people, "a chosen race," "a royal priesthood."
There you, without losing your unique identity, are in and
among a people, a saved nation, a people of God's promise;
you are a person, precious and unique, whose claim to God's
redeeming love rests on your presence within a people. You
can think of yourself as belonging to a church, but the meaning of church is "people of God."

The point of all this is simply to suggest that you must
not get too wrapped up in yourself when you wrap yourself
in prayer. Never let your speech in prayer betray you. You
cannot, and must not, permit yourself to try to go to God
alone. Yet you are the world's leading expert on your own
needs, hopes, and dreams, and God is delighted to hear
about all that (even though God knows your thoughts before
you speak) directly from you.

Let me nail down this point with a true story about a
practice followed by a member of the admissions committee
at one of our nation's very best law schools. She was a faculty member and one of a dozen or more members of the
important committee that decided who would and who
would not be admitted to that particular school. She told me
that the first (and sometimes only) thing she did when the
applicant's file was placed before her was to read the personal essay. If no other person was mentioned in that essay—

no teacher, coach, role model, parent, friend—no other person who had touched the applicant's life in some significant way, if the perpendicular pronoun *I* dominated the essay, the entire file was set aside and rejected.

"What I do is not unfair," she explained. "A dozen other readers will go through the entire file and if I'm the only negative vote, the applicant will get in. I just refuse to have any thing to do with adding another narcissistic, solipsistic, self-centered, selfish, ungrateful, egotistical person to the ranks of a profession that has all too many of that kind of person already!"

God will surely be a kinder judge. But even God will be a better listener if mention is made of the needs of others, the gratitude one has to others, and the joy of journeying with others through this life on our collective way home to heaven.

CHAPTER THREE

Stages

"All the world's a stage," Shakespeare has Jaques say in Act II, Scene VII of *As You Like It,* and this famous speech continues with the words: "And all the men and women merely players. / They have their exits and their entrances, / And one man in his time plays many parts, / His acts being seven ages."

Ages for some; stages for others. There is progressive, if uneven, movement through the ages and stages of life for everyone.

I've listed six stages for consideration in this chapter. Shakespeare lists seven "ages." First "the infant," second the "whining schoolboy," and then "the lover," next "a soldier," the fifth age is "the justice, / In fair round belly with good capon lined, / With eyes severe and beard of formal cut." The sixth age "shifts into the lean and slippered Pantaloon / With spectacles on nose and pouch on side." The seventh and final age "That ends this strange eventful history, / Is second childishness and mere oblivion, / Sans teeth, sans eyes, sans taste, sans everything."

No such thing as "mere oblivion" for the believer, even though the firmest of believers might feel him- or herself "sans" almost everything but faith as one's personal, possibly "strange," and surely "eventful history" draws to an end.

The embers of faith are always there. Faith abides through all the ages and stages of life. They are there, ready and waiting to be fanned into the flame of prayer. And faith enflamed into the dancing forms of prayer sustains the praying person with a supportive spirituality at any age, in every stage, of life.

You, my reader friend, can identify and label the stages of your own life. You can also arrange the ages, decade by decade, or year by year, as you noticed in chapter 1. You can sequence them for reflective processing in prayer. You can shuffle them for solitary review the way the player lays out the cards.

It is interesting to reflect on the various meanings and images that come to mind with the word *stages*. Rebels stage a coup. Soldiers gather in staging areas. There are early and late stages in the history of a particular illness. "Onstage" means on display, exposed to view, and this extends to being "on a stand," which further suggests the link of stage to standing, to state, to status, and even perhaps, to stagger, where one loses his stand and falls. Each stage of your life puts you at the ready, so to speak, ready now to act, and, as a person of faith, confident that there is always another act yet to come. The curtain may fall, but the play goes on forever.

We all make many exits and entrances; we all play many parts, assuming, of course, survival into adulthood. We walk and run, stand and fall. We posture. We wear many masks. We pass in and through, back and around, up and down the stages of life. And for each of us there was a beginning, an unremembered day, but a date never forgotten—the date of your birth.

Birth

Nine months is a long time. Ask any mother. Or, to get a fresh perspective on the duration of a pregnancy, think of the normal school year. In terms of elapsed time, you completed your freshman year (or the duration of any one elementary year of schooling) before you were born! And the unremembered experience of your own birth is something you would probably want to forget anyway, if the sounds and sights were somehow now available to memory.

You made it. You arrived as a direct result of the love, sacrifice, nurturing, patience, skill, and pain of others. That unique other, your mother, alone felt the pain. Notice how the simple addition of an "m" identifies her as the unique, nurturing "other" who gave you birth. It was for you an unrepeatable experience. She had a role to play at a privileged stage of her life. She managed your first entrance— kicking and screaming—onto the stage of life.

I've made occasional visits to the Neonatal Intensive Care Unit of the Georgetown University Hospital. I looked in on the septuplets born there in July 2001. I've seen many infants struggling there to connect with life outside the womb. And I've admired the skill and compassionate care of the nurses and physicians whose commitment and skill amount to life support for newborns grasping for a hold on life. Any infant inspires awe; every infant, either healthy or in need of special help, depends on others for survival.

Every infant struggles in speechless dependency. Any newborn is the center of significance in his or her unfolding life—warm or cold, wet or dry, hungry or satisfied, held or not—a developing infant consciousness measures all surrounding influences in terms of meeting or failing to meet the unarticulated needs of self.

You, my reader friend, were there once. The distance from there to here is one measure of your indebtedness. So, you might be inclined to pray:

Thank you, Lord, for the gift of life.
Thanks, too, for your gift to me of those who
*   cooperated with you in giving me life.*
Before I had any capacity at all to understand,
*   I experienced the meaning of love.*
Before I had any idea of what it means to trust,
*   I somehow trusted others.*
You entrusted me to them.
You, who hold my destiny in your hands,
*   entrusted me to their care.*
I can name my mother and father, and naming
*   them now, I beg your blessing upon them.*
I cannot even name those who assisted at my birth,
*   but I beg your blessing on them too,*
*   and on all who do that labor of love today.*
As I reflect on my origins, on my own birth,
*   Lord, I beg you to give me a deeper and*
*   abiding respect for life. And I ask you to invite me,*
*   now, in this reflective moment,*

into a silent reflection of the wonder of birth
and the meaning of life.
Words are unimportant now, and so I continue
to pray in silent wonder.

So put this book aside now for another time. Just think. Just listen. Just pray.

Childhood

Shakespeare saw this as the age of the "whining schoolboy." Your childhood, spent in school, in "Playland," or "Toyland," or any other venue of "sweet little girl and boy land," is a stage you were probably anxious to leave behind, but to which, if the experience was positive, you are happy to return now in memory. Your childhood experiences were shared, of course, but your own memories of childhood are unique to you. What is your earliest memory? Does it open you up or shut you down?

Harper Lee's 1960 novel, *To Kill a Mockingbird,* deals with fairness, civil rights, and social justice. It is also, a psychiatrist who works with children told me when the book first appeared, "the best nontechnical exposition of the workings of the six-year-old mind" that he had ever seen.

You may remember the little girl, Scout, coming home after her first day in the first grade and announcing to her lawyer-father, Atticus, that she was not returning to school—ever. Why? Because the teacher told her she had to unlearn the way her father had taught her to read.

"[R]eading was just something that came to me....I could not remember when the lines above Atticus's finger separated into words, but I had stared at them all the evenings in my memory, listening...to anything Atticus happened to be reading when I crawled into his lap every night."

In an effort to get her to reconsider, Atticus reasoned with his daughter this way: "If you can learn a simple trick, Scout, you'll get along a lot better with all kinds of folks. You never really understand a person until you consider things from his point of view...until you climb into his skin and walk around in it."

As the story unfolds, Scout does indeed learn to "climb inside the skin" of others, especially two "mockingbird" characters, each innocent, harmless, and vulnerable, who are done in by an unjust and brutal society.

The first half of this novel portrays a nostalgic growing-up experience in a small Alabama town. The second half disposes of small-town Southern gentility to expose the harsh reality of prejudice and ignorance in ordinary folk. If part one can be called "The Education of a Little Girl," the last half of the book could be labeled "Racism Runs Deep." It did then, in the story setting of the 1930s; it still runs deep today. Racism is a form of learned behavior, however, that wouldn't run anywhere without first having been taught.

The child in this novel learned a lot about racial justice from her father. Her adult recall of how she "crawled into his lap each night" recalled as well the lessons learned there. Her brother Jem learned a lot too from a wise father. "The one place where a man ought to get a square deal," says Atticus to Jem, "is in a courtroom, be he any color of the

rainbow. But people have a way of carrying their resent-
ments right into a jury box."

If values are "caught, not taught," as some learning
theorists suggest, these children heard words from their
father's lips, but learned the lessons from his principled
behavior. As you take a moment now to recall parental
words and actions that helped to shape your own convictions and character, take this one last morsel of nourishing
food for thought that Atticus passed along to Scout:
"[B]efore I can live with other folks I've got to live with
myself. The one thing that doesn't abide by majority rule is
a person's conscience."

Children learn the "rules of the game" on playing fields
and game boards, by sitting around card tables and camp-
fires. Their schoolyard contests and after school conversations are often punctuated with shouts of "No fair! No
fair!" And they often learn from the personal experience of
injustice how to be themselves more just to others.

Roam or run now through the avenues, paths, hiking or
biking trails of childhood memories. Many memories are
waiting for you there on the street where you lived, the
house of worship you came to know, the theaters, gyms,
lakes, beaches, libraries, museums, and relatives' homes you
visited. And let those memories lead you into prayer that
might begin like this:

Thank you, Lord, for making childhood part
    of your creative plan.
I'm grateful, too, now that I stop to think about them,
    for all those big people,

who, I realize now, did not so much hem me in
as open me up.
Memories of my childhood world are good and bad,
happy and sad,
but mostly happy and good because those
generous elders were there for me.
Thanks, too, for the other kids. Even the bullies
and the taunts who later learned,
I'm sure,
from their own mistakes, and who never
really threw any "sticks and stones."
Instead they childishly relied upon unkind
words that, in fact,
"never hurt me," and have
faded now from memory.
There were, of course, some childhood hurts, but I
survived them.
I'm grateful now for your healing grace.
I'm grateful for the resiliency you, in your generosity,
lavished on me,
letting me learn in the process the wisdom
of generosity,
the importance for growth
of a little encouragement,
and the indispensable gift of another's belief in me.

There is a line in the Broadway play *Hair*, the musical
that brought a new dawning of the "Age of Aquarius" to the
turbulent 1960s that has Claude saying, "I believe in God,
and I believe that God believes in Claude!" So may it always
be for you through childhood and all the stages of life.
Believe that God believes in you!

Youth

In her famous *Diary*, Anne Frank wrote that in its innermost depths, "youth is far lonelier than old age." Not everyone shares that experience. Some are more likely to associate turbulence rather than loneliness with their adolescent years. Now there's a word that almost shouts out "rocky terrain." Contrasted with the gentle sound of the words *child* and *childhood, adolescence* provides acoustical agitation that points to turmoil within. Sometimes that turmoil can be productive; it can produce character. Take for example the fictional character who portrayed genuine character, Mark Twain's Huckleberry Finn, the embodiment of adolescent integrity.

Recall for a moment the predicament in which Huckleberry Finn found himself in the fictional but down-to-earth world of rafts, rivers, and runaway slaves. Huck has integrity and authenticity. He is genuinely incorruptible. Recall the fix he found himself in. He was helping Jim, a runaway slave, to gain his freedom. The law said that Jim was property; he belonged to Miss Watson. According to the law, Huck was stealing, taking something that didn't belong to him. In befriending a black man and in treating him as an equal, Huck was acting contrary to both law and custom. Huck had been taught that Jim was not his equal. Huck had internalized the dominant public opinion about the institution of slavery—it was not only acceptable but the quite proper way of doing things. But he began to believe that slavery was wrong; he felt stirrings in himself that prompted him to reject a way that he knew deep down to be unjust and immoral. But it wasn't easy. Listen to him agonize:

> *"The more I studied about this the more my con-*
> *science went to grinding me, and the more wicked*
> *and lowdown and ornery I got to feeling....It*
> *made me shiver....I was a-trembling, because I'd*
> *got to decide, forever, betwixt two things, and I*
> *knowed it. I studied a minute, sort of holding my*
> *breath, and then says to myself: All right, then, I'll*
> *go to hell."*

And that, of course, marked a break for Huck from both law and religion insofar as they supported the institution of slavery, which he, in his heart of hearts, knew to be plain wrong. "It was awful thoughts and awful words," Huck adds, "but they were said. And I let them stay said; and never thought no more about reforming." Better, perhaps, if he had said, "never thought no more about *conforming*" to unjust laws, to inhuman institutions, to unexamined and unfair social conventions.

Mark Twain's wonderful novel is an indictment of a society that accepted slavery as a way of life. Twain puts Huck and Jim together on a raft as sterling examples of integrity, so much more moral than those "proper people" on dry land. Huck offers the reader an example of courage to live life according to principle; in this case a principle of loyalty and fundamental justice. You act on what, in the depth of your being, you judge to be the right principle no matter what the Miss Watsons of the world think of you, no matter how the prevailing public opinion judges you.

Now this is not to suggest that law is to be disrespected or disregarded in the period of adolescent self-discovery. It is possible, however, to use the law as a substitute for responsible decision-making, and as a shield against growth-producing choice. Many adolescents, along with armies of morally underdeveloped adults, do just that.

Conformity is part of the air that young people breathe, and some never outgrow it. Dress, slang, "in" and "out" places to be, movies to see, persons to know—conformity sets the standard of selection. Not so for Huck Finn. Not so for many principled people who made it through adolescence by sinking their roots into personal convictions—the right ones.

While I was teaching at Georgetown during the 1990s, a young policeman friend, who saw more than he wanted to see of youthful irresponsibility, remarked to me, "If I were you, I'd tell those kids: 'Turn that cap around, pull up your pants, and get a job!'" Most of them did, shortly after they took their diplomas and ran off into the "real world."

I don't remember when they started turning their baseball caps around so that the visor shaded the back of the neck instead of their unfurrowed youthful brows. J. D. Salinger's *Catcher in the Rye,* who was, of course, a high school boy named Holden Caulfield, may have started that fashion. He started a lot of other things that lasted through the entire second half of the twentieth century. If you ran a frequency count through the pages of that 1951 novel, you'd come up with "phony" so often that you might begin to believe that the over-thirty crowd was an army of moral nomads in empty suits. But the moral of the story seems instead to be that Holden was just a casualty of the adolescent narcissism that is there, like a trap, awaiting every unsuspecting youth.

So think about your own adolescence, your high-school days, your youth extended out as far as your definition of *youth* allows. And let your thoughts lead into prayer:

*Everyone can say, "I'm not as young as
    I used to be," and when
I now say those uninspiring words, Lord,
    I admit I'm making excuses.
I'm not a kid anymore, and I guess
    I'm now a poor excuse for what the
    kid I once was might have become.
I'm not a "has been," I know, just
    a "might have been."
But don't let me come down too hard
    on myself for that, Lord.
Nobody's perfect. There's no one alive who
    could not have done a better job.
My youth wasn't wasted, just insufficiently utilized.
You created me with infinite potential. Infinity is still
    out there in front of me: life unending with you.
No end. No limits.
My youthful foolishness and sinfulness are
    well known to you, Lord.
I thought I had no end, no limits then, in this
    life, during my youth. Or so it seemed.
I know better now.*

And so I say I'm sorry for not appreciating
the gift of youth more,
for not better developing my potential,
for failing to plan, and pace, and prepare.
Forgive me, Lord.
But, as I say, don't let me come down too
hard on myself now.
I was just a kid, a youth.
Tell me that my foolishness made you smile.
Tell me that my future is secure.

Even though you may have done your best to extend the boundaries of adolescence beyond all previously established limits, adulthood eventually welcomed you into the ranks of the mature. On now, to the next stage.

Adulthood

Consider the widespread devaluation of the word *adult* in the contemporary American vernacular. An anecdote will help to make the point.

A foreign graduate student from India arrived a few days early to begin a program of study at the University of Scranton. He had preregistered for courses and knew the books he would have to purchase. On a walk around town, just a few blocks from campus, he noticed an "Adult Bookstore" sign, walked in, and was astonished at what he found. Welcome to America! Enjoy your stay with us! Just don't expect to find serious textbooks in a store specifically for adults!

Adult entertainment. Adults only. We don't have the vocabulary to label properly our immature fascination with erotic images and ideas. Uneasy about giving youngsters easy access to these materials, we post the "adults only" sign to exclude children and welcome those with sufficient size and weight dimensions to pass unchallenged through the door, but insufficiently endowed with the character and emotional maturity required to stake a claim on the title "responsible adult."

Adult is, after all, a wonderful word. Adulthood is, in truth, a special trust. Think a bit about what it really means to be an adult. You're free now of the "mind-forged manacles" that may have tied, if not locked you up in childhood fears. You should be free of impulsive activity. Prejudice should, by now, have relaxed its grip on you. You are autonomous, not totally independent, just autonomous—a free-standing adult capable of relating disinterestedly to others, putting others' interests ahead of your own, serving others. You are free to choose; that means freedom to choose wisely or not well. You can choose self-service and self-enclosure, or you can choose to have regard for others, to be compassionate to others, to live for others.

Only an adult can begin to understand the meaning of sacrifice. And only sacrifice can unlock the deepest meaning of love.

Heroic sacrifice is found typically, if it is to be found at all, among adults. And more adults are heroes than give themselves credit. Some dive into icy waters to save the drowning. That is heroism. Some run into burning buildings to rescue the injured and dying. That is heroic activity also. In a sense, the real hero is someone willing to sacrifice his or her life for another. You have to be a genuine adult to be capable of that. But it isn't just that once-and-for-all, split-second, heroic self-sacrifice that is the stuff of adulthood. There are countless adults who lay down their lives for others day by day—for spouses, for children, for elderly parents, for helpless and needy human beings. They prove themselves capable of meeting adult demands of smiling self-donation. That's what it means to be an adult!

Adulthood is a special stage of life, a sacred stage, a happy stage, a stage from which a higher life is launched. Physical diminishment will set in. Adult controls will unravel, but only to wrap up a life for that later stage of aging. So, while you're thinking about that, take a moment to pray.

What a gift it is, Lord, this life you've given me.
What a privilege it is to be an adult—fully formed,
responsible, ready, willing, facing up to the
challenges of life.
But, as you know, I always think I'm not quite
there yet;
there's an "older crowd" that has been setting the
pace for me since I was ten.
I'm a pace-setter too now; I know, but I'm not
convinced of that.
I'm so aware of how I come up short.
Let me grow—not "up," as I used to pray, or
"taller," as I dreamed of being—
let me grow deeper in adult wisdom.
Free me up to be more empathetic and understanding.
Teach me to be generous, and through my
generosity may I prove to myself that I am
at last really an adult.

*And what a joy it will be when I can honestly
say "amen" to that!*

Old Age

The words *old age* fall with a thud to the floor of human consciousness. Once they apply to you, there's no going back;
that's for sure. Nor is there any prospect of another stage
ahead in the span of years that is yours. Once you're old,
you're old—boxed in, contained, physically framed, limited.

Optimism tells you that "the best is yet to be." But real-
ism reminds you that "yet to be" means not to be experienced in this world. Faith would have you not forget that
you are going to live forever. But old age finds you forgetting
a lot of things including, on occasion, your faith-based conviction that you will indeed live forever.

There is only one door that leads you into life everlasting, and you keep backing away from that door.
Understandable. Natural.

You have to take a moment from time to time to look
at that reality from God's perspective. The table is set. The
banquet is ready. It's not so much that your "number is up"
as it is a case of the invitation having been sent. They're
waiting for you. "They" in the sense of the God who created
you, those who gave you life, who educated and nourished
that life in its earlier stages, and who have gone on before
you: They are all waiting to welcome you home.

And you don't want to go. Understandable. Natural.

You may have gone through all the earlier stages of life
thinking of God as a big impersonal umpire just waiting to

call you "Out!" at the plate, when, in fact, God is there waiting to welcome you home. That's a perception problem and it is your problem, not God's. You can work on that problem in your old age. If you work on it to the point where others might notice, the evidence will probably not surface in the form of external piety on your part, as much as it will be the suggestion of internal peace, a certain mellowness resident within you somewhere behind a smile. Serenity. Confidence, which, of course, means "with faith." That's the kind of old age that you, with God's help, can build for yourself.

You'll need the help of others. Caregivers will be there for you. Be nice to them. Be grateful. Family will be there, if you are blessed with family. If not, God will be there for you; you can count on God being there in and with your family and friends, and, if there are no family and friends, God alone will be there for you so that you will not be alone.

When old age finally catches up with you, you are approaching your birthday, which may still be years away, but is coming nonetheless, your birthday into heaven. Happy Birthday? Why not?

Just as your birthday into this world was surrounded by welcoming hands and open arms, your birthday out of this world will carry you into a new welcoming environment of love. You haven't been there yet, so how can you be sure? You haven't yet gone through the door, so how can you know what you are going to find on the other side? You can't know these unknowns (but not unknowables) as you've known so much through all the earlier stages of your life. Now, in this life, you can know these realities only by faith. Only faith can convince you of this. Your faith can carry you through.

Old age is a proving ground for faith. It is faith's garden, laboratory, or library—whichever metaphor you prefer. You've got work to do—cultivation, experimentation, reflection, prayer. This is privileged time, not to be polluted by worry or glazed over and dulled down by mind-embalming entertainment (although entertainment that respects both your dignity and your intelligence should be very much a part of your experience of old age).

There is joy in old age. And there is sadness too. Sadness overcome by brave efforts to reassure the younger ones that there is dignity in old age is constructive sadness; it is a contribution that only those who are old can make.

There's been a widespread secular heresy at work in America for a long, long time. It convinces the unreflecting that "what you do is what you are, and if you do nothing, you are nothing." Dead wrong. So destructive of the human spirit; so damaging to self-esteem. We are, all of us at every stage of our respective lives, human beings, not human doings. When old age makes it more difficult or even unnecessary "to do," no one, least of all the person who is old, can retain a claim on his or her humanity and succumb to the callous conclusion that it is, therefore, no longer useful or necessary "to be."

Old age is just another stage of life. And like every other stage in life, old age offers both content and context for personal prayer.

"Lord of all ages," cathedral choirs sing.
"O, God our help in ages past," we sometimes sing and
pray.
I'm wondering now not about the ages of the earth, or
the ageless Creator of it all;
I'm thinking about myself and the cubicle of my life that
bears the label "old age."
Is it for me an achievement or an outcome?
Is it something that has already happened or is about to
happen to me?
I have to think about my freedom in accelerating,
delaying, or denying its approach.
I'm unsettled, Lord, even frightened by the absoluteness
of the category.
I'm not saying older, or elder, or aging; I'm saying old,
and I'm saying it of me.
When, Lord? How long, O Lord?
At every stage of life you've been there for me, Lord.
I know I can count on you; I just hope that you can
always count on me.

Death

When you consider death as a stage—an end stage—of life, you cannot escape thinking about your own death. Speculative thoughts of death in general, of what the moment of death might be like, of how those who have gone before actually went—all this is an interesting and by no means unproductive or morbid reflective exercise. But here in these pages, in the framework of the sequence of stages in your life, you cannot avoid facing up to the fact of your own death. It is coming. You are going to die.

"I'm sorry, but your time has expired! Have a nice day!" That message popped onto my computer screen after I went to the "Death Clock" site on the Internet and dutifully filled in my day, month, and year of birth, and noted my sex. I didn't notice that the last blank was filled in at the default setting of "normal." Had I scrolled it down to another option, "optimistic," I would have had my lease extended to April 24, 2023, and could have taken comfort in the assurance that I had "679,323,918 seconds to go," whereas the "normal" exit had my ticket punched seven months before I even went to the keyboard and made the inquiry!

All in good fun, of course, just another pastime provided by your computer. Past-time or pass-time? Both I guess. You can pass time reflecting on these things. That upon which you are reflecting is waiting for you out there, somewhere, past your time. Meanwhile, have a nice day!

My friend Abigail McCarthy once wrote of the "parade of life." She used that phrase in reflecting on "love and abiding friendship, the mystery of children growing and changing, the joy of intense thought, the gift of books and teachers of many kinds, the human capacity for simple fun, the pleasure of shared comfort and warmth, the great multiplicity of the people of this earth with whom one can be in some kind of communion, the simple wonder of the colors, and the sounds of the parade of life." For Abigail the colors went momentarily dark on February 1, 2001, as the sounds went silent and the parade stopped at the door of death. She stepped into eternal brightness, unending songs of praise, and life eternal. For the rest of us, the parade goes on.

The fact of death underscores what Karl Rahner called the "unrepeatable onceness" of life. Reflection on death can, therefore, gently nudge us toward a greater appreciation of the day in and at hand, the present moment, the gift of right now. There is an unrepeatable onceness to it all.

Rahner, the great German Jesuit theologian who died in 1984, replied to a question about whether or not he feared death by saying, "I have the right as a man, a Christian, and a theologian to be afraid of this dark event...I hope to have the strength to surrender lovingly into the great Mystery of God's love which embraces it." He also suggested that you can anticipate death by practicing renunciation, "by enduring loneliness, silence, and perhaps by forgetting oneself."

That surely gives you a lot of material for prayer, so give it a try from time to time (while time lasts!).

Heavy stuff, Lord, and more than a little on the dark side too.
I've got to face up to the fact of death, and I don't even want to begin thinking about it.
Don't let me be too rough on myself now, Lord,
*   but hold up my heart as I admit to my arrogant insensitivity to the gift of life.*
It has been all gift and I have not been all grateful.
I'm not saying I haven't been at all grateful, just not all-grateful,
*   consumed with gratitude, for the precious gift of life that is mine.*
Nor have I been consumed with respect for life in others.
I've taken it all so much for granted. Living as if I'm going to live forever (how foolish can you be?).

*Unmoved at the death of others, that's me (not unaware,
     just unmoved).*
It is all so uneven and uncertain.
I don't want to go suddenly; I don't want to linger either.
*I don't want to leave a mess behind for others to clean up,
     but I can't get myself organized to tidy things up.*
*May I have the good sense now, ordinary common sense,
     to tidy myself up:*
To say, "Sorry" to those I've hurt.
To say, "I forgive you," to those who hurt me.
*To say, "I love you," to those I do indeed love and have
     failed to say so often enough.*
*To say, "Come to take me, Lord, when you are ready;
     and in your coming, ready me to come to you."
     Amen.*

CHAPTER FOUR
Circumstances
❧ ❧

Sickness

Sickness is not simply the other side of health; it is an unavoidable part of the human condition. When you were young, very young, it meant trays in bed, a lot of extra attention, and a good excuse for missing school. It may also have meant, in those childhood years, unmanageable anxiety produced by pain, the proximity of needles, and the awful taste of medicines. But there it was—part of life. And there it went, along with all your cuts and bruises, out of a body restored to health and into a mental archive far from the fresh air and sunshine of childhood activity.

Sickness came to parents and grandparents, to playmates and their parents. Hospitals became recognizable as having a special purpose among all those other big buildings of life outside the home. Sickness was seen, if not intensely experienced, for what it always will be—a part of life.

At later stages in the life cycle, you may have begun to notice disease and widespread illness in other parts of the world. Prevention strategies—personal and societal—

engaged your attention to some extent. Closer to home, you found yourself making visits to comfort and reassure friends and family members temporarily confined to hospital beds. You hoped you would not fill future vacancies in those care-providing units, but you knew the possibility was real. You know from newspaper accounts and the experience of others, if not your own, that accidents happen, and you do your best to avoid them.

When illness strikes, whether it be the common cold or cardiac arrest, you ask, "Why me?" and you wonder where things went wrong. After-the-fact resentment arises where before-the-fact resistance might have played a preventive role. You may even be, shameful as the admission may be, envious of those who are not ill. But there you are, sick and in need of help. Medical help will be foremost on your mind. If you think about the need for spiritual help, you might seek it in words like these:

Be with me, Lord. Be with me in my anxiety, my pain,
  and my discomfort.
I need you by my side.
Why me, Lord? Be gentle as you let me know.
When will this pass, Lord? Let me draw hope from your
  reply.
Is this the beginning of something worse? Sustain me
  with your grace no matter what.
Don't let me envy those who enjoy good health; just
  let me put my trust in you.
Let my trust be anchored in you,
  as I entrust myself to caregivers.

Let me see them as the instruments of your love for me.
Guide their hands and make them the instruments of
    your providential care.
In their gentle touch, let me see your "strong right arm."
Be with me, Lord. I am lonely and afraid.
I need you by my side.

Words like these can help. With or without words, you can breathe in God's presence, God's love; breathe out your anxieties, your fears, and your worries. In many moments of prayer, you should let yourself breathe in God's love and then simply breathe out your thanks. This rhythmic breathing prayer—love and gratitude—will take on a life of its own. It will produce a stabilizing effect. It will restore calm in choppy emotional waters.

Dear reader friend, you know by now that I am a Catholic priest writing here neither for Catholics only nor for Christians in some exclusionary sense. But it is only natural for me to write from my Christian-Catholic experience, and I might be expected to draw explicitly on that experience in instances where it might be helpful to anyone who holds this book in his or her hands, anyone who uses these pages as a path into prayer.

This reflection on prayer in time of sickness is one such place.

There is a special Mass for the Sick in the Catholic missal or "sacramentary," the altar book used by the priest in offering Mass. Here are the words of the opening prayer in that Mass for the Sick:

Father, your Son accepted our sufferings
to teach us the virtue of patience in human illness.
Hear the prayers we offer for our sick brothers
and sisters.
May all who suffer pain, illness, or disease realize
that they
are chosen to be saints,
and know that they are joined to Christ in his
suffering
for the salvation of the world.

No need for me here to get into a discussion of a Christian perspective on the redemptive power of the sufferings of Jesus. The point to be made for all who believe in God is that the sick are "chosen to be saints," that the all-powerful God who created this world out of nothing can, in a way that remains mysterious to us, *do something* with the nothingness that is the absence of health. Something good for you and for this world can come out of your sickness. That's what saints do—something good for themselves and others.

As unwelcome as your illness may be, and as implausible as it may sound to you in the midst of "pain, illness or disease," you are called to be a saint!

Nonetheless, we pray for your restoration to health. And you are expected to pray also for good health. In that same Mass for the Sick, the priest prays:

God our Father,
your love guides every moment of our lives.
Accept the prayers and gifts we offer
for our sick brothers and sisters;

restore them to health
and turn our anxiety for them into joy.

Any sick person would surely be willing to say "amen" to that!

Similarly, the closing prayer in that Mass for the Sick will be music to the ears of any Christian and, except for the reference "to your Church," a congenial request presented to an all-powerful God on behalf of any sick person of any faith commitment:

God our Father,
  our help in human weakness,
  show our sick brothers and sisters
  the power of your loving care.
In your kindness make them well
  and restore them to your Church.

Made on behalf of yourself or anyone else, that prayer invites a warm "amen" from any believer. It, along with the words from the other prayers quoted above, offers something of a script to be followed by anyone at all that wants to turn to God in prayer in time of serious sickness.

Health

Unless you are a hypochondriac or chronic invalid, you tend pretty much to take your health for granted. Even when hospitalized, you think good health is an entitlement and you look forward to your reinstatement back where you belong—in the ranks of the healthy.

Faith sees good health as a gift. Reason views health as part of the harmony of nature. Break the balance of nature or violate its laws, and you can expect to pay a penalty in the precious coin of health. Faith and reason together acknowledge the presence of a higher power that can protect and prevent, as well as heal and restore, in the matter of the maintenance of human health.

A corrective for our tendency to take anything for granted is gratitude. When you let gratitude come into play in your life, you are welcoming a transformative influence. It can alter your perspective; it can change your life. In the old American vernacular, *much obliged* was an everyday expression of gratitude, a folksy way of saying *thanks*. Reflection on the content of that expression can introduce a sense of obligation into the awareness of the one who has reason to give thanks—an obligation not only to show one's gratitude, but to use one's gifts and giftedness in the service of others.

"Much obliged," Lord, for my good health.
In prayer to you today, I say thanks for the gift of health.
I also ask your pardon, Lord, for doing less than I should
        to maintain my health.
Thanks for food, and rest, and the ability to exercise.
For all those things that are "good for me," I give you
        thanks.
You are the source of everything that is good;
I am the recipient of so many good things, including
        health.
So, while I'm brimming with health,
I want also to pour out my thanks.
I know my good health won't last forever.

But while it lasts, Lord (and may it last a long, long time),
*   I hope to use it wisely for your glory and generously*
*   in the service of my brothers and sisters in the*
*   human community.*
For the health I enjoy, and the happiness it brings with it,
*   I thank you, Lord.*
I declare myself to be "much obliged."

There is much more to health, my reader friend, than "my health"—yours or mine—of course. You are well aware of that. And even if you've had only one eye open over the past couple of decades, you surely will have noticed that there's been a revolution in healthcare in America. Not only the revolution in molecular biology, pharmacology, and medical technology; we've also had the Human Genome project, the possibility of gene therapy to cure genetically inherited disease, new surgical procedures, wonder drugs. There is also the revolution in healthcare delivery and insurance.

I heard a molecular biologist remark a few years ago that relative to the future of medicine, "We are today where Wilbur and Orville Wright were in 1903 relative to the future of air and space travel!" Where will medicine and healthcare be in another one hundred years? We need God's help to guide us into and through an unknown future that is full of possible cures for human ills, full of the potential for preventative measures against disease, but also fraught with ethical dilemmas concerning what we can and should do, and what we simply must not do by the laws of God and nature, in using new knowledge and new techniques.

And there is more. The managed-care revolution, which is still going on, has changed healthcare insurance and delivery. There are the twin questions of cost and coverage. Outlays for healthcare, as a percentage of gross domestic product, are enormous. As a result, other social needs are not being met. Mounting expenditures for end-of-life care divert funds from preventative care in the early childhood years. Insurance coverage is expensive and incomplete. With an estimated forty-four million uninsured persons in our country, how can we regard ourselves as serious servants of the common good?

What can you say to God, and how can you say it, in the confusing context of health insurance, healthcare, scientific research, and medical experimentation? All you can do is try because in all of this the stakes are so high you cannot afford not to bring your concerns to prayer.

Stand by me, Lord.
Give me courage whenever illness strikes
and, in health, give me a firm commitment to do
what I can to build a sane and secure medical future.
Stand by our scientists, Lord.
Keep them mindful of their need to obey the laws of God
and nature as they explore the mysteries of both.
Stand by our policymakers, Lord.
Let them see the needs of the medically indigent and
make provision for them.
Let them acknowledge that not everything that can
be done should be done;
but inspire them to encourage research even when
research results might have to be contained.

Bring the policymakers, the ethicists and scientists,
    the theologians and physicians together—heart to
    heart, mind to mind—to walk the path of progress
    according to your will.
Stand by our healthcare providers, Lord.
Deepen their commitment to care and
    help them to understand and follow the highest
    ethical standards.
Let their hands be your hands in the art of healing,
    their eyes your eyes in seeing medical need here
        on earth,
    their feet your feet in walking among the sick and
    restoring them to health.
Stand by our healthcare insurers, Lord.
Let them serve rich and poor, young and old.
Let them realize their role in the promotion of justice in
    our world
    and resist the tendency that all of us have to put
    personal gain above the common good.
And finally, Lord, stand by and with us all
    in the face of human decline when healthcare can
    no longer help,
    and only you can sustain our hope and give us life
    unending.

Riches

In the movie *Wall Street,* actor Michael Douglas spoke a famous phrase that has lodged itself into the minds and memories of millions of Americans: "Greed is good."

Labor leader Samuel Gompers, a few generations earlier, spoke out of a related but more measured mindset when he answered the question, "What does labor want?" with the monosyllabic reply, "More."

It seems we always want more. And for many of us, greed is, if not altogether good, then not so bad that it can't serve to get our engines running in the race for riches. We like money. We enjoy income and, if we can accumulate it, wealth. Nothing wrong with that, we say. But then we wonder why we find ourselves talking to God about money only when we need it. We tend not to bring it to prayer when we have it, and we have to wonder why. Could it be the fear of being nudged to share it? Facing God with hands full and pockets deep might prove embarrassing. Could it be that we are blinded just a bit and less open to listening to God when we are flush with cash and secure with wealth?

There is a story in nineteenth-century rabbinical literature that has an unhappy but wealthy man approach his rabbi for advice and help. How to find meaning once again in his life? How to find happiness? The rabbi walked him across the room to a window. "Look out and tell me what you see." "I see people walking up and down the sidewalk below." Then the rabbi led him toward a mirror on the wall of his study. "Here is a looking glass; take a look and tell me what you see." "I see myself."

"Ah," said the rabbi. "I am sorry to have to compare you to these two types of glass. Notice the only difference is that one has a coat of silver on one side. When you were younger and less well off, you could look out on the world through clear glass and see others, and reach out to help them. Now your outlook is covered over with silver. You can no longer see others clearly. You do not think to reach out to them and meet their needs. If you want to be happy again, scrape away some of the silver in your life. You will be able to see others again. You will find happiness."

Lord, can you possibly understand me when I pray:
  "Make me a silverscraper"?
I really don't mean that I want to scrape together
  a pile of precious silver shavings.
I just want to scrape away whatever it is that is
  closing me in on myself.
My spiritual vision needs sharpening, and there may be
  some kind of celestial carrot juice that I can take.
But even with twenty-twenty spiritual eyesight, I'll never,
  without your help, see through the wall of stuff that
  encumbers me, or around the piles of possessions that
  weigh me down.
I'm surely not ready to take first prize in the
  giveaway derby, but neither am I altogether unfeeling
  and self-absorbed.
Let me feel for others where they hurt
  and share with others when I should.
And if this should prove to be my road to happiness,
  let me put myself on record as saying I think that
  would be just great.

Poverty

I tend to think of poverty as "sustained deprivation." It can be voluntary or involuntary, sustained over a long period of time or relatively brief in duration. It can be good for the soul (and sometimes for the body too), or it can be crushing of the human spirit and destructive of the human body.

Poverty is the condition of millions of my brothers and sisters in the human community, more than I could ever count, many more worldwide than there are those who enjoy the good things of which those who are poor are deprived: food, clothing, health, shelter, education, longevity.

Poverty exists around the world and, sometimes, even around the corner. Too often, I just don't see it.

As I ask myself, Lord, of what are the poor deprived,
I also have to ask, by whom or by what, is their
deprivation caused.
Am I in any way the cause?
Am I complicit in the societal mechanisms that work
against the poor?
Is injustice in any way at work in all of this?
Is it "necessary" in any pernicious way for some
to be poor so that others can be rich?
What can I do to help, Lord?
What must I do, if I am to be a contributing member
of the human family,
a responsible citizen in the community of persons
and nations on this planet?
I don't expect direct replies to these questions, Lord,
I just ask that you give me the gift of awareness—
seeing problems where they are, and the gift of
compassion—reaching out when and where I can,
and the gift of faith strong enough to know that
you are somehow there in the poor waiting for me
to find you there.

Poverty touches you and me at times in ways we often fail to understand. I'm not talking about being a poor golfer, poor cook, poor loser, or poor correspondent. I'm not referring to the fact that both your manners and your memory may be poor at times. These are all deficits that you can live with or adjust. Whether we use the word strictly or loosely, *poor* can lead to serious considerations of human dependency. Poor health comes to mind. Poor prospects for future employment. Poor performance in a high-stakes test.

You've heard an oft-quoted observation, "I've been rich and I've been poor, and rich is a whole lot better." You get the point. You also may be familiar with a Wall Street adage, "When the bears are running, it simply means that the money is going back where it belongs!" Whether you've participated in or just observed "paper losses," you know that a "here-today-gone-tomorrow" threat hangs over just about anything you have to call your own. Poverty in any shape or form can remind you of your contingency, dependency, and the fact that—tax collectors and undertakers aside—there isn't much that's certain in ordinary human experience. Not much maybe, but surely not nothing at all.

I have faith, Lord.
It is not of my own making; it's a gift for which I'm
grateful.
I have faith enough to walk over my "underwater
options." They literally and figuratively don't count
now, Lord, but you always do.
Whatever poverty I know, whatever shape or size my
deficits take,

I have you, Lord, to sustain me.
My net worth in your eyes is eternal
even when there's no more life in my physical and
financial assets.
Faith tells me this is so, and I believe.
Lord, root me by faith in the things that are eternal
so that
I can sit loose in life to the things of time.
In poverty, I see dependency on you.
In you, I can find a way out of any deprivation.
Of myself, I can do nothing;
with you, and in your unfailing love for me,
I am rich beyond all imagining.

Frailty

With the lengthening of the life span in America, we hear more frequent references now to the "frail elderly." They "get around," and seem to manage "on their own," but they are at risk of falling. They are more vulnerable to infection and accident. He or she is "slipping," some will say of another person, and the observer is not thinking of icy pavements or banana peels. When you hear that your friend in some distant place has "failed" over the past year, you know that you are not receiving news of an academic transcript, driver's test, or business venture. You are in touch with the inevitable.

We spend the first half warming up and the second half wearing out. That's life. "We're on the back nine now, my friend," remarked one acquaintance of mine to a friend of his recently. "I'm on the nineteenth hole," the friend shot back, "and it's not all that bad."

Indeed it isn't bad. It is all part of life. And, just as things "go better with" (fill in the brand name of your favorite beverage), this part of life goes better with faith.

Faith, however, does not automatically kick in for you in the senior years. They don't ordinarily program faith into "Elderhostel" courses. You may not have reflected much on faith, its reality or its precepts, in earlier, more robust years.

"Faith in action" sounds great, but most active people pay insufficient attention to the importance of faith in their lives. Like water, it has been there all along, beneath the surface, seeking its own level, seeping through, following you all through the years. But if you neglected consciously to stretch out your roots in the direction of the water of faith, you might now be a bit dry, even brittle, in your elder years.

Frailty is part of eldership. Faith is part of frailty.

Water can help. Think of those pools or ponds that are often part of assisted living programs; think of their buoyancy, their gentle invitations to move the limbs and stretch the muscles. If you observe those 10:30 a.m. "workouts" in the water at retirement communities or assisted living centers, you'll notice that the elders no longer splash; they simply move gracefully against the friendly resistance of the water. And in the process they gain strength.

Lord, strengthen me in my frailty.
I'm not seeking miracles.
My medals, ribbons, and trophies are on the wall or
*   in the case.*

I'm not thinking about returning to competition.
I'm not hoping to sprint again, or catch a pass, or ace
a serve.
I'm just asking for graceful acceptance of frailty,
accommodation to limits.
I hope you'll help me remain steady on my feet.
I look to you, not dimly as through a windshield at
night, but clearly with the eye of faith.
I can still see down the fairway.
And I wouldn't mind at all if I could see you as my partner
on a quiet round of chip-and-putt,
with no more at stake than gratitude for now,
and a twinge of regret that I wasn't more conscious
of you
"being there" for me when I was hitting the longer
ball and scoring well,
and doing it in what I foolishly thought was all
"my way" completely "on my own."

When we who are on the short side of eldership are completely honest with ourselves, we have to admit that we look at frailty as failure. Somehow or other they failed to stay in shape, failed to keep their strength, failed to eat right, exercise regularly, and retain their vigor.

You might as well say that they failed to pick the right parents and then connect intravenously to the fountain of youth. Values of the youth culture dominate entertainment and advertising and thus work their way into our view of the world. People used to say, "It's a man's world," and they were thinking of athletes and economic success stories. Then along came *Woman's World* magazine and a lot of effort to

even the scales in the popular perception of achievement differences between the sexes. But the subtle conviction remains
deep in both the male and female heart that ours is a world that
belongs to youth. Once you're over a given age-determined
hill, you are an irrelevant spectator on the sidelines of a passing parade. You may have raged against sexism and racism;
now you think about joining forces with those who want to
take on ageism.

Young or old, Lord, we belong to you.
We are your people, whether limber or limited, spry or
*   slow of foot.*
Some of us think quickly; others find our arteries closing
*   early and opening late.*
Young or old, Lord, we belong to you.
When we are no longer young but not yet old,
*   we tend to think a lot about ourselves and less than*
*   we should about you.*
Thanks for your patience, Lord; thank you for ignoring
*   my ingratitude and gathering me up in your*
*   forgiving and understanding arms.*

Strength

When you were a child, did you ever invite an elder to "feel
my muscle?" Little boys and girls alike, but mostly boys, will
extend an arm, clench a fist, bend an elbow, and stare at the
slightest hint of a bulging bicep in the upper arm. "See how
strong I am!"

Boys at play (perhaps girls as well; I don't know) like to
adopt "strong" names. "Call me Steve" was a familiar request

in my own childhood circle of friends that included no one named Stephen. "Bobby," "Billy," or "George" just wouldn't do it. Neither would "Jimmy" even in those days of tough-guy Jimmy Cagney movies where the hoodlum was the hero and the cops often objects of ridicule.

"Let me carry him" (usually a younger brother). "I can lift it" (often a piece of porch furniture). We can all recall our participation in claims or demonstrations of physical strength in those tender years before we ever heard of hernias. The strength myth (strong man, strong woman, strong arm, strong will, strong statement, strong medicine) persists to the point of locking our minds and emotions into some kind of "strongbox" to which we have lost the key that will open us up to tears, admission of error or defeat, and an open declaration that we stand in need of help.

I love these lines from Carl Sandburg; they make you think of working-class Chicago in the 1920s and 1930s:

Those who order what they please
when they choose to have it—
can they understand the many down under
who come home to their wives and children at night
and night after night as yet too brave and unbroken
to say "I ache all over"?

Bravery is sometimes prideful ignorance, and ignorance can leave one "blissfully unaware" of where the real dangers lurk. Strength is virtue and virtue is strength. The virtuous person will become strongest in the broken places.

O, God give me strength.
I don't mean to be disrespectful, Lord, but as I hear
myself saying,
"God give me strength," I can't help thinking of, and
hearing my exasperated mother react to a
broken cellar window, or to a large hole dug
behind our house in the first stage of a children's
tunnel project intended to connect Philadelphia
with Peking.
But strength I need and so I pray, Lord give me strength.
Strength for today; strength for all the days ahead.
Strength to deal with not knowing how many days I
have ahead.
Strength to apologize; strength to say, "I'm sorry."
Strength to say, "I love you."
Strength to put up with pain,
with being overlooked,
with insults and ingratitude.
I gladly leave the barbells to others, Lord.
I flex no muscles, just move my lips to say, "Lord
give me strength."
Heal me in my broken places.

Success

Who can define it? Who can say for sure that success has been achieved? In many situations, success is a goal without a goal line. All too often, without really thinking about it, we drop a vertical line through each "s" in the word success and measure the meaning of the word in terms of financial gain. Pile it up. Stash it away. Whoever has the most at the end of whatever game you happen to be playing, wins.

But is that what it's all about? And isn't it just a bit arrogant to say, even if you say it only to yourself, "I'm a success"? Is it a curse or a compliment that the high school yearbook bestows on the smiling senior designated as "most likely to succeed"?

Remember hearing someone sing (or hearing yourself singing), "What's it all about, Alfie?" You may have given that question some thought along the way. "What's it all about when you sort it out, Alfie? / Are we meant to take more than we give?" There's a lot to sort out when it comes to measuring success. And I have yet to find a "how to achieve it" or "how to attain it" book that even suggests that giving more than you take is a formula for success.

"Nothing succeeds like successors" is a refreshingly candid way to assess oneself and one's achievements when "stepping down" from a position of responsibility. We sometimes say "stepping aside" at transition time, but we never say "stepping up" to a new level of freedom from recognition, fame, power, and responsibility—from "success," as we tend to understand it.

You've been advised to "dress for success," and you've probably made more than a few expensive additions to your wardrobe by way of acting on that advice. Some automobile manufacturers would have you believe that you can drive for success—the more expensive the car, the higher you rise in the esteem of those who observe you at the wheel. And you've been encouraged to get a toehold on the "ladder to success" and waste no time climbing to the top. But only you can tell yourself if that ladder is up against the right wall!

Success is in your own mind. That's where it should be. Not in the minds of others. Not in the goals others set for you. Not in the expectations others have for you. The expectations you have for yourself are important. But you can be a victim of the promises you make to yourself. They, like the expectations you set for yourself, can exercise a tyranny over you. Let you own good mind "sort it out" for you. Reflect on the elements that you would typically associate with success and let your mind assemble those elements in a balance that is right for you. Money will be part of the balance. So will reputation and the esteem of others. Health, friendship, and love for and from others are all part of the balance. Measurable achievements will be part of the balance too—outcomes, results. All of these are part of the picture of success that belongs in your own mind; that's where you measure success.

There's a biblical verse that helps you tie it all together: "Give success to the work of our hands," sometimes translated "prosper" the work of our hands (Ps 90:17). Whatever it is, success, the success that God will give to the work of your hands, is the balanced combination of things that can only be good for you. Pray for that when you pray for success. Wrap your mind around that, and don't trouble yourself with thoughts of what others might think success for you should be.

Please, Lord, give success to the work of my hands.
Those hands were formed by you
and, like the mind and heart you also formed for me,
were given to me for a purpose.

I know I'm a human being, not a human doing, but I was
    born to do many things.
No need to apologize for that. Why else would I have
    hands and mind and heart?
Let me do well in everything you would have me do,
    and let me not be drawn to do that which you would
    not want me to do.
Let me do for others—generously and competently—as I
    do for myself.
And let the symbol of my success be a smile that says,
"I did the best I could, and what I did,
I did for the love of God who gave success to the work
    of my hands."

Now, my reader friend, let me ask how you might know if
that prayer was "successful." Did it work? Has God given
success to the work of your hands?

The only way you'll ever know, this side of heaven, is if
you find yourself smiling a smile of success. Not faking it.
Just finding it on your face—a smile that says all the elements are in balance. You're OK. You just know it because
your mind says it's so. You can say it: "Success." And you
can't stop that word from ending in a smile.

Failure

You've often heard it said that success has many fathers,
while failure is an orphan. There's a lot of truth in that.
There is, of course, no "orphanage" anywhere in the world
providing a secure environment for those who consider
themselves to be failures, no safe haven protecting and

enabling them to "grow up" and reach success. If there were such a place, the whole expanse of the earth would hardly be large enough to contain it.

Most people, men in particular, consider themselves to be failures. Even those you'd least suspect of having anything less than total confidence in themselves and complete satisfaction in their personal achievements—even they often believe, in their heart of hearts, that they've been doing it with smoke and mirrors, "getting by" somehow, not letting on that they regard themselves as failures waiting to be discovered.

In a culture that puts the premium on success, the productive side of failure is, more often than not, overlooked. You can learn from your failures, your mistakes. You have to own up to them, of course, and admit that you goofed before the learning process can begin.

Humility can enroll you in the school of recovery from failure; once enrolled, there is much there that you can learn.

One singularly important lesson is that failure is an important part of most success stories. It is, however, a preamble or foreword, not by any means the full story. Failure can launch the success story only if the person who fails first reflects on the experience of failure, and then makes a fresh start. In fact, the greatest failure of all is the refusal to take a risk in the first place—the failure to give it a try.

In the words of Robert Browning, "a minute's success pays the failure of the years." And that, I think, can be understood in either of two ways. You pay for success in the coin of failure, even repeated failures, on the way to success.

Or it can be said that a single success makes up for many years of failure. The problem that those burdened with failure have to face up to is that it takes a lot of heart to "try, try again."

Of this you can be sure: If you refuse to lower your net, you will catch neither fish nor failure; you will be stuck all alone and lonely not on, but with, yourself. Hope has a way of helping you deal with all this, as you will see in the next chapter. Courage also has to come into play when failure makes your spirits sink. For now, just think a bit about failure as you know it in your own experience, and turn your thoughts toward God:

Help me unscramble my thoughts, Lord, as I think about failure.
The root meaning of the word says "fall" or "fault"
to me, but it isn't always my fault
when things go wrong; sometimes it is, but not always.
And as for falling, wouldn't "falling in love" or "falling into a great new job opportunity" be an example of success, not failure?
So, I guess I need your help in taking a positive approach to failure.
Don't let me get down on myself, or better, help me not to let myself get down on myself.
Is it possible to separate myself from my failures?
Not in the sense of dodging responsibility,
or in the sense of separating my doing from my being.
Somehow or other I have to come to understand that I am not my failures; I am me.

And I can become a better me through the failures from which, by your help, I can emerge to give it another try. That word emerge *gives me the hint of resurrection, and surely you know a lot more about that than I do. But emerge I will, by your gracious help, to leave failure behind and to walk with you on the path of true success.*

Doubt

It is difficult to convince people that doubt does not disqualify them from the community of believers. To have doubts does not condemn you to lifelong skepticism. To waver now and then in your convictions does not make you a moral nomad or a rudderless voyager on your way home to heaven. Everyone has doubts, lots of them.

I'm not saying you can never be sure about anything. And I'm certainly not saying that it is normal to go through life without any strong convictions, even though it sometimes seems that we, as a nation, run the risk of being convicted in the court of history of having no strong convictions at all! Not everything is up for grabs; not everything is a matter of opinion. Relativism must never be the rule.

I think it would be hard to find a more honest prayer than the sentence put to Jesus by a man who asked the Lord to cure his son who suffered from convulsions. The father said to Jesus, "...if you are able to do anything, have pity on us and help us." Jesus said to him, "If you able!—All things can be done for the one who believes" (Mark 9:22–23).

Then the boy's father said these wise and memorable words: "I believe, help my unbelief" (Mark 9:24).

Each one of us needs help in managing our burden of unbelief, in living without doubts. Make that prayer your own, "Help my unbelief."

Funny, isn't it, how our conversations are so often punctuated with "undoubtedly," "doubtless," and "no doubt." Those words suggest a surefooted certainty that more often than not simply isn't there. I think of them as the conversational equivalent to "whistling in the dark," the age-old deflective device of overcoming fright by letting others think that you feel quite safe.

Accept your doubts. Don't let them paralyze you, or worse, destroy you. "Do it!" is the command every doubter has to heed. Otherwise, the lock clicks on your inaction and hesitation rules the mind. Doubt can result in the theft of freedom. That is something to pray about.

*Lord, you know me better than I know myself, so you
    surely know my doubts.*
*I'm not asking you to banish them, just to help me
    manage them.*
*I guess doubts are the dues I pay on my membership
    in the human race.*
*No increase in dues would be appreciated, naturally, but
    I know that mental doubt, along
    with physical decline, is part of being human.*
*Faith is the only way to deal with doubt, and I do look
    to you for the gift of faith.*
*There is no stopping physical decline—delaying maybe,
    but no halting the process.*

There is no total avoidance of doubt. Help me to
    understand that.
And help me to manage it by keeping all my doubts in
    perspective.
They can never outweigh your love for me.
They can never dislodge your presence in my life.
They can never smother the belief I have that I am secure
    in my belief in you.

Certainty

The "death and taxes" answer to the question of whether or not anything is certain doesn't even come close to the mark. And voices representing fundamentalist religious extremes are nothing short of frightening when they make assertions about certainty.

Where do you look when you look for certainty?

First, I think, you have to look to yourself. You have to look within your mind and heart. Life has a way of influencing both mind and heart in the matter of certainty. It also has a way of protecting mind and heart from getting trapped in false certainties. Live long enough (and it doesn't have to be all that long) and you'll have some certainties. You can count on them to be there for you every time.

Some of your certainties are other people. You can count on them. Like you, they have changing moods and thoughts, but deep down, you can count on them. They are there for you. Viewed in this light, certainty is another name for love. Love can disappoint. Love can die. But in your own experience—somewhere within you—you know certainty in your love for another and in that other's love for you. You can count on it.

Other certainties are yours in the realm of ideas. They are always there for you. They provide you with an interpretative framework; they enable you to sort things out. There is mathematical certainty. There is measurable, tested, scientific certainty. And there is a common-sense certainty available to all, but sometimes more noticeable in simple, uneducated folk, who have experienced enough of life to come up with sure and secure ideas.

Then there is the certainty of faith. Take this opportunity to free yourself of the "seeing-is-believing" fallacy. You know what you see. You know it based on the evidence of sight. You don't "see" what you believe, but you know it nonetheless. You know it on the authority of another. I can tell you something about my childhood home and, based on my testimony, you take it to be true, even though you never saw the place. You know something because I told you. Because you take me to be a reliable witness, you are certain of what I said.

The best witness of all, of course, is God. Do yourself the favor of taking God's word, properly interpreted and understood, as a basis for some certainties. And let those certainties sustain you in your transit through life. Faith-based certainty is not fundamentalism. Because faith is pure gift, the certainties that flow from faith must be tempered by gratitude, which, in turn, rests on humility. Out of that humility, offer a grateful prayer to God for the certainties that are yours.

Lord, God, I know that I exist,
*   and I believe in your existence.*
Because that belief in your existence is based on your
*   word, communicated to me in scripture,*
I now say that I know you exist even more surely than
*   I know that I am here.*
Of that I am certain.
I thank you for the other certainties in my life.
In the quiet of my heart,
*   where only you and I can hear,*
*   let me pause to enumerate them now.*
Certain persons are certainties to and for me.
For them I give thanks, as I mention them by name.
Certain ideas are certainties in my mind, matters of deep
*   conviction.*
For them I give thanks, as I jot them down on the notepad
*   of memory.*
Let me be certain, but not arrogant, Lord,
*   understanding, but not intolerant.*
And I pray that you will permit an increase in the supply
*   of certainty in our world that is matched by a*
*   decrease in both arrogance and intolerance in*
*   our times.*

Loneliness

Loneliness is surely a circumstance associated with all
stages of the human condition. It is a universal experience.
No one of us was made to be alone for long, although we
may at times choose to be. Solitude and loneliness are quite
different realities. Solitude is a chosen form of isolation.
Loneliness is an unwelcome separation from human inter-
action.

For some, loneliness is a disease. For others, a predisposition. For still others, a temporary condition with a ready exit. The door out is a genuine concern for other people. Become more interested in what you can do to ease the burdens of others than with what they can do to ease yours, and you will find your own burdens, especially the burden of loneliness, lifted. It never fails.

Many years ago I tore a sheet from The (London) Sunday *Times* Magazine Section (May 27, 1962) and put it in my files. The page-wide single-word headline reads "LONELINESS," and here are several paragraphs from that article:

> You don't notice them. Loneliness is a disease without physical symptoms. Only the victims know they suffer it: the bleak sensation of walking alone through a world of other people's friends. There is no clear sign of loneliness in the pretty girl idly window-gazing in the High Street, alone; the middle-aged shabby women lingering in teashops, alone; the dark, scattered figures in the Sunday afternoon cinemas, each alone; or the old men and women who blossom suddenly on park benches in the first spring sunshine, to sit waiting and watching for conversation, alone. You don't notice them, but there are more of them now than there have ever been.
>
> The number of lonely people in Britain has been rising steadily for the last twenty years. Today, general practitioners, psychiatrists, and social workers recognize it as an alarming iceberg of social malaise,

in a country which is becoming steadily more impersonal as its mobility grows....

In the dictionaries, solitude and loneliness are the same thing; in life they are not. Obviously, everyone needs some time to hear himself think. Some people are natural solitaries, content with their own company; or, if they believe they have one, with that of their God. Writers, painters, composers, require more solitude than most; heavy responsibility must to some extent set a man apart.

But loneliness is not a chosen form of isolation. It is a sense of deprivation: the emptiness of the human being who longs for contact with others but who is, through circumstance or temperament, denied it. Solitude is an interval in living, but loneliness is a kind of death.

The famous *Diary of Anne Frank* carries this entry for Saturday, July 15, 1944: "'For in its innermost depths youth is lonelier than old age.' I read this saying in some book and I've always remembered it, and found it to be true."

Forced under Nazi persecution in 1942 to go into hiding for two years in a house in Amsterdam, this young (she was born in 1929) Jewish girl died in 1945 in Bergen-Belsen, a German concentration camp. Her story is unusual but not unique. Her *Diary* is a tribute to the courageous spirit of young and old alike who died under Nazi persecution. Her belief that the pain of loneliness is more acute for the young is open to debate, of course, as we think about nursing homes and assisted living facilities. The point is not to be argued here, just remembered in the face of troubling statistics relating to the alienation of youth and the frightening reports of youth suicide. As disease, loneliness can be deadly. But, as troubled elders will attest, it can also be chronic.

There is probably no one who ever prays who has not taken his or her loneliness at one time or another to prayer. You, my reader friends, don't really need me to prime the pump. Too bad that I can't provide all my readers with a convenient way of exchanging with one another phrases and prayer-notes on this theme out of your own experience. Do that if and when you can. Meanwhile...

I keep thinking there is no one here but me, Lord, as
     I turn to you in prayer.
But I know that isn't true.
My thoughts and words rise up to you out of a world
     filled with people.
I'm lost in a population mass of billions of people.
I'm surrounded on every side with human beings like
     myself.
I'm deafened by noise generated by humans.
I'm dazzled by the speed of human activity.
And yet, somehow or other, none of this is touching me.
It is not reaching me.
What is touching me is the pain of loneliness.
How can I be so alone, so separated?
Apartness is one thing.
Privacy is another.
Individuality is not all bad.
But loneliness?
Have you condemned me (or have I condemned myself)
     to being alone?
How can I break out of this box, Lord?

Speak to me, if you will.
As I make that request, I wonder whether I should be
*   speaking up and out to others.*
Not to myself, and not just to you, but to others.
To others who might be waiting for my call.
To others who might be lonely too.
Speak to my loneliness, Lord, and I know you will be
*   speaking to the real me.*

It would be fun (I've never attempted it, so I'm just speculating) to run an Internet search or do a frequency count of the number of times the word *lonely* crops up in American popular music. Country music might lead the pack, but the count would be high in show tunes, "middle-of-the-road" music, rock, and all the other forms that can be heard, hummed, or sung aloud. Lonely lives abound; lonely notes make their way all the time into lonely hearts. Lonely people tend to feel sorry for themselves. Not so for those who choose solitude.

Solitude

This is a chosen form of isolation, solitude. It is not to be avoided, even though the prospect might be frightening. It is to be chosen as an environment within which both depth and growth come to the human spirit. Those who neither know nor cherish solitude confuse it with loneliness and, more often than not, presume that it is associated with sorrow. Solitude is an environment of happiness.

Peace is part of the environment that is solitude. Death and dying are not. One might face death peacefully in solitude, but that is quite different from facing death alone. In a certain sense, everyone, even those surrounded by loved ones at the moment of death, dies alone. Sadly, many facing death are lonely and afraid. But, if I may be permitted to make the point once again, loneliness is not to be confused with solitude.

So it makes a good deal of sense to practice solitude often during life, especially during the prime years of life. Apartness, separateness, quiet reflection—all of these are conditions you can choose to make your own. If you do choose them, you grow as a human person.

You need others, of course; you are social by nature. But you bring a better self to meet, and live, and be with others, when you come to others out of the experience of solitude.

You can find God in solitude. Indeed, that's the reason many men and women of faith turn to solitude. They want to be alone with God. Something deep in the human spirit yearns to be with God, to be alone with God. You, my reader friend, can reflect on your own experience, review your inclinations, retrace your steps, and I'm sure you'll come up with memories of quiet moments, moments of apartness that might even have lengthened into days of consciously being alone with God. Those were times when you chose solitude. Only you can say whether or not they were qualitatively different from periods of loneliness. I'll bet they were! In your loneliness, you may have come close to convincing yourself that God was far away and out of reach. In your solitude, you know—by faith—that God is at your side. So turn to God from time to time, in solitude. And talk to

God about what is in your heart. And then listen to God speak to you in silence, and most memorably, in solitude.

Lord we meet in solitude—mine, not yours—in solitude
   we meet.
Solitude is for me a chosen form of isolation.
I choose it not just to be more consciously in your
   presence;
I choose it to be more centered on my existence in your
   world.
Light, not darkness, accompanies my solitude.
Light sweeps out my fears and opens up the avenues of
   my mind.
I think more clearly in solitude, even though I need others
   to help me shape my thoughts before and after I begin
   weaving them in solitude.
Thinking isn't all I do in the blessed circumstance of
   solitude.
I just let awareness surround me there, awareness
   that I am loved and that I love, awareness that I am
   held secure by you, awareness that I am blessed with
   the love of others in this world, awareness that
   countless others have gone before me here,
   and countless more are still to come.
So out of my solitude rises prayer for others—those
   I love, those who have gone before, and those yet to
   come. They all are yours, Lord, and they are also
   somehow mine. I am somehow part of them.
Only now am I coming to realize that in solitude
I can more readily notice myself to be in solidarity
   with all who ever lived, and all who are to come.

Embarrassment

A generation ago, college students writing home for more money had to remember that there are two "r's" and two "s's" in the word *embarrassment*. Today, financially strapped students tend to use their cell phones, where spelling is not an issue. But as e-mail finds its way more and more into family communication, attention will once again have to be paid to the r's and s's.

There is much to be embarrassed about in both the written and oral communication of otherwise well-educated young people today, but this is a book on prayer, not pedagogy. (I can hear some now saying that only prayer will cure the communications ills that afflict the young and challenge their educators! But that is a matter to be treated outside the covers of this book.)

Have you ever been asked to recall your most embarrassing moment? What passes for television entertainment occasionally exploits those memories. Teenagers sometimes delight in trading them. But our reflection in this area right now should be both private and analytical. Behind the memory there has to be the question, why? Why was I embarrassed? Can embarrassment tell me anything about myself? Does embarrassment provide me with anything to bring to prayer?

Ignorance can protect a person from embarrassment. If you don't know you are saying or doing something stupid, you will hardly be embarrassed by whatever you might do or say that raises the eyebrows of others. If you have neither a sense of modesty nor of shame, you will not know embarrassment in circumstances that are certain to produce it in others who have both standards and sensitivities.

Embarrassment can put you on the path to humility. It can pull away your ego props and cause you to question, and rightly so, your presumption of self-sufficiency. As much as you would like always to think of yourself as self-assured and in control, an embarrassing moment can reveal your vulnerability.

Let your embarrassments remind you of your incompleteness, your dependency on human support, divine help, and hard work. Let them also remind you of your membership in the human race, where all are fallible and no one is perfect.

Be sure to reflect as best you can on what should embarrass you and does not. Manners and modesty may have receded to a position of noninfluence in your decisions and behavior. Try to complete sentences that open up along these lines: "I'd be embarrassed to have to admit...." "This probably should embarrass me, but it doesn't, because...." And then take it all to the kind of quiet prayer that takes place when you close the door, and pray in quiet to the God who hears you in quiet, knows you, and wants you to be embarrassed only by the things that separate you from him, and wants you never to be embarrassed to open your heart to him in self-disclosing prayer.

Lord, I'm embarrassed to say so, but...and...but....
You hear the cry of my embarrassment, I know.
You are so good to me.
You know me, as I am, and love me for that.

*Help me to come out from behind my many embarrassments
and begin to believe that you believe in me.*
*Help me to stop using embarrassment as a way of shying
away from you and closing in on myself.*
*Let me change so that my most embarrassing moments
will be those moments when I doubt your love for me.*

Insight

It happens every now and then. You "see," you "get it," you
"understand." That's what insight means. You see into an
idea or into a person. You reach in with your mind. You
grasp a satisfying portion of meaning.

All of us are searching for meaning all the time. One
way of describing or defining spirituality is to view it as forg-
ing connections, throwing a bridge of meaning over different
realities and thus connecting them in your mind. What could
be more different than you and God? Spirituality helps you
negotiate that difference and close that gap.

You almost always find yourself saying "insight into"
when you use the word *insight*. You get insight into yourself,
insight into your problem, insight into the mysteries and rid-
dles of the human condition.

An insightful person is always to be admired. Insight
associates itself with wisdom. "Pain make man think,
thought make man wise, and wisdom make life endurable"
is an insight communicated by the elfish Sakini to the atten-
tive audience in *Teahouse of the August Moon*.

Strictly speaking, you do not gain insight when you
learn a fact or discover a previously unknown place or per-

son. You do in those instances gain knowledge and some immediate understanding. Insight requires excavation. You probe for meaning. You search not simply for facts, but for connection between the facts. Your thought runs toward the inferential and the abstract. You discover previously unknown or unnoticed relationships.

It should be easy, then, to come to an appreciation of the need for insight in order to probe the depths of self, the roots of meaning, and the hidden wonders of the world, the mystery of your hidden God. Scholars toil to gain insight into ordered reality. But insight has a way of leaping over the disciplinary boundaries and the steps of ordered inquiry, important as those measured movements of the mind are. Insight simply "sees it," "gets it," and "grasps it," all of a sudden, in a flash, in an instant.

"The man of God welcomes the light. So that all may see that his deeds are true." Those words introduce the "Office of Readings" in the Liturgy of the Hours for Saturday in the Third Week of Lent. Light is associated with insight, which often comes "like a flash."

The test of your integrity, of your transparency, if you claim to be a man or woman of God, is your openness to the light. Many of us preserve a protective corner of darkness in our lives; we don't always welcome the light. That is understandable, but deserving of investigation.

All of us have a lot to be humble about. Some shameful things may be part of the baggage we lug with us through life (even though it has been tossed long ago into the infinite ocean of God's merciful forgiveness). Insight into all of that can be the foundation of true humility, a true personal humility. And a substantial spiritual structure can be built on the ruins or personal pride and arrogance. Yes, we all have a lot to be humble about, but that simply means that we all have the makings of a firm foundation for personal integrity.

The only thing that can destroy that foundation is hypocrisy. Pretend to be someone or something that you are not; teach, preach, or say one thing and do just the opposite; live a lie. There you have the formula for hypocritical behavior. If hypocrisy warns you not "to welcome the light," then not all "your deeds are true," and only you and God know how vulnerable you are to discredit and disgrace if that searchlight illumines your corner of darkness. This realization can open you up to a two-tiered prayer.

Lord, let me make an act of faith in your forgiveness.
Let me never be shaken in my belief that you have healed
  my brokenness and made me whole.
But likewise, never let me fool myself.
Never let me be a hypocritical fool who lives a lie, who
  needs forgiveness, and does not admit it.
So I pray for insight into my potential for doing just that;
  insight also
  into the evil of being double faced and double minded.
But most of all, I seek insight in positive directions.
Let me "see" your love.
Let me "grasp" your goodness.
Let me "know" beyond a doubt that you are God and I
  am yours.
Let me "realize" the goodness that is within me
  and "recognize" its source in you.

*And let me "meet" you in the goodness of others today
and always. Amen.*

Discovery

For reasons explainable by my age and early education, the
word *discovery* always makes me think of Christopher
Columbus. Had I been born, say, in the 1990s and was
invited now to react to *discovery* in a word association
game, I would in all probability come up with "The
Discovery Channel." The word means different things to
persons of differing experiences.

For those who have experienced difficulty in life on the
way to gaining knowledge, insight, success in one's calling,
or the wisdom that comes, as we say, with age, discovery is
an achievement, not an accident.

For those who "strike gold" with relatively little effort,
discovery is more like winning the lottery—a matter of luck.

For all of us, regardless of age or experience, dis-cover
means removing the veil. It involves uncovering what otherwise would remain hidden. Lawyers speak of the "discovery stage" of preparation for trial, or they advise clients
that certain files and records are "subject to discovery,"
meaning that they must be produced, brought to light,
when requested by counsel for the other side in an adver-
sarial proceeding.

Anyone associated with a *cover-up* lives in fear of discovery. Anyone who explores the unknown hopes to enjoy
the thrill of discovery. Discovery leads to progress. It pushes
back frontiers. It opens up the future.

Once in the outpatient area of a Veterans Administration hospital, I heard a technician ask a veteran waiting to have blood drawn whether he knew what his number was—a reference to the system of taking a number to get a place in the line of patients waiting for service. "I know all my numbers," replied the Vietnam-era vet. "I just don't know who I am!"

Self-discovery is a personal pursuit as old as human consciousness. Rarely achieved to anyone's full satisfaction, the "know thyself" goal is a universal human concern. Psychoanalysis aims toward greater knowledge of self, to insight into one's deepest drives and desires. Unaided personal reflection on the "who am I?" question makes philosophers of us all.

Religion requires self-knowledge as a prerequisite for anyone to be truly religious, to be, in other words, grateful to the Creator-God, repentant of personal choices that fended off the love of God, and conscious of one's redemption by an ever-faithful God. And at the bottom of the depth of religious experience is the recognition of oneself as a sinner, a loved sinner to be sure, but a sinner nonetheless. From the depth of that awareness, one can rise, by God's grace, beyond the stars. Now *there* is a voyage of discovery! Prior to departure, however, take a moment or two to pray.

Lord of everywhere and everything,
Lord of all creation,
Lord of all insight and awareness,
Lord of all that is hidden and unknown,

Lord of all my comings and my goings, of all my "been
  there's," and "done that's,"
  be also Lord of all discovery for me.
Let me grasp with the eye of understanding an ever-larger
  portion of the knowledge
  of the ages.
Let me gain from the school of experience,
  an ever-wider awareness
  of the best in human experience.
Let me see with the eye of faith you, Lord, as the ultimate
  object of all desire and discovery.

CHAPTER FIVE

Moods

‿◠ ◠‿

The word itself will put your mind in gear. Think about moods and you begin to hear music, see familiar scenes, and find your memory running from pain to pleasure, sadness to joy. Play with that word awhile and you will move away from song titles and facial expressions, down the path of grammatical niceties like "subjunctive mood" (meaning a "mode" of expression) on to "modal" references to form rather than substance. Moods shift; modalities change.

"There is a kindly mood of melancholy," wrote the eighteenth-century poet John Dyer, "that wings the soul and points her to the skies." Moods can carry you up and down and all around. This chapter offers roadside rests for your wandering moods, or take-off points and landings for the moods that soar, or safe harbors for moods that meander through your mind like rivers running toward the sea.

Let melancholy, which is another word for sadness, serve now as your point of reflective departure.

Sadness

Everyone knows what sadness is. But not everyone can recognize its roots. "The saddest words of tongue or pen are these four words: It might have been." I've heard that verse, or variations of it, quoted many times and saw it attributed to both John Greenleaf Whittier and Oliver Wendell Holmes. It points to regret as a root of sadness. You can't upend the hourglass and let the past sixty minutes begin all over again. You can't delete the text and rewrite the script of your life. You can, of course, "try, try again" in the absence of success, but every deed has a way of remaining done, buried in the world of "what might have been."

Sadness enters your life through other doors as well. High hopes are not infrequently a prelude to deep disappointments; hence the importance of keeping your expectations within a reasonable range of reality. Insufficient preparation sets you up to fail the test; hence the need to respect the demands that preparedness will invariably make on you. Loss of loved ones, loss of property, loss of reputation and self-respect are sometimes unavoidable, but the sadness-producing impact of loss can be mitigated by a healthy spirit of detachment. "Fixed as he was in the things of eternity," said an admirer of the late Jesuit theologian Gustave Weigel, "he could sit loose to the things of time." Sitting loose does not mean not caring; it simply means caring most deeply only about the things that last forever.

Chesterton noticed of the Irish that "all their wars are merry and all their songs are sad." Sad songs touch the heart and linger in the memory as if to cushion the blow of adverse circumstances and assure the one whose heart is heavy that he or she is not alone. It is presumed that there is comfort in knowing that these sad things have happened before to others. The "wars" of our various activities and campaigns tend to distract us from our troubles and can lead to the false conclusion that happiness is a function of hyperactivity. If sadness sets in when you turn the engine off, you have to wonder whether the person you call *you* is a human being or a human doing!

Sadness is more a matter of not having anyone to share with, rather than not having much to share. Materialists have difficulty appreciating this. The remedy to sadness, they think, is more of the measurable, tangible, bankable, wearable, consumable, enjoyable goods and services an economy can produce. The "bads" of everyday economic life can make a national product really gross. Reality requires you to live with both "good" and "bad." Wisdom suggests that service, not "services" in the economic sense, is a good route away from sadness.

Become more concerned with how you can serve, with what you can do to lighten the loads of others, and you will find yourself a whole lot less concerned about your own burden. You will, in other words, find yourself leaving sadness behind.

Lord, you know my sunrises and sunsets,
my ups and downs, my highs and lows.
If, as the hymn-song says, you are the "Lord of the
    Dance," let me say that you are also the Lord of the
    foot-dragging, sad-sack brigade with which
    I sometimes plod along.
But I know it doesn't always have to be that way.
I can pick up the pace when you pick up the drumbeat.

You invite me, I know, to hold my head high.
You expect me to reach out to others.
When I have the courage to do that, I know I will have
    found a remedy for sadness, perhaps not a perfect
    and lasting remedy, but a real good start on the road
    to higher ground and happier days.
And to these few thoughts, let me say, now and always,
    amen.

Joy

I taught long ago at a college named Loyola—Loyola College in Baltimore. A friend and faculty colleague would often bring his young children to campus for sporting events or liturgies. One of the youngsters always called the place "Joyola." Now, many years later, I'm back at Loyola and I can still hear that happy child shouting out "Joyola" as his own joy found expression in hops, skips, and jumps on campus lawns.

Somehow or other, joy gets into your feet even before it finds its way to your face! Of course, as we grow older, our joyful moods find different modes of expression.

Discerning persons know the difference between joy and pleasure. Recognition of that difference is an early sign of maturity. With wisdom comes the understanding that even happiness and joy are not the same experience. It is possible to have deep-down joy beneath surface unhappiness, although, more often than not, external signs of happiness will accompany an inner awareness of joy.

Think of things you enjoy doing. Think of persons whose company you enjoy. Think of food and drink that you

enjoy, possessions you enjoy, achievements you enjoy recall-
ing, stories you enjoy retelling. What can you discover there
at the root of these enjoyments? More often than not, it is
someone or something present, not absent, to you that serves
to explain your joy. So savor the notion of presence as you
search for the meaning of joy.

If the presence is you, the joy will not last long. Even
you can only take so much of yourself! If the presence of
someone or something—in person or in memory—enhances
you, enlarges you, adds to your store of value, the enhanc-
ing, enlarging reality will bring a joy that is directly propor-
tional to your recognition of that reality as gift. Recognize
the source as gift and then let yourself be grateful. The gratitude must touch your being, if your being grateful is to last.
And forgive me for emphasizing the obvious, but here it is:
The root of your joy relates to both presence *and* gratitude,
specifically to your gratitude-remaining-present to your consciousness!

Men and women of faith find joy in the presence of the
God who created them, who graces them now, sustains and
encourages them, affirms and accepts them—no matter
what! There are times, as each of us knows in his or her
heart of hearts, when neither affirmation nor acceptance is
deserved. Nothing at all surprising in that. How else can
grace be understood if not as something totally gratuitous,
as something completely undeserved? Gratitude to the giver
is your only possible response. And joy is inevitably associated with this gratitude. That joy brings balance to your life.
The joyful person cannot help but be a balanced person. And

here are words a balanced person might want to speak to
God.

Lord, God, creator of everything, including me,
I can be nothing but grateful to you and in my gratitude
    I find joy.
Balance is also there within me in your presence.
For me balance and joy are inseparable.
Hilarity and sadness would unbalance me, seesaw me up
    and down.
Anxiety would keep me off balance.
But joy, balanced between the high of loving you and the
    low of forgetting that you love me, keeps me together,
    on balance,
    in your presence,
    in your love.

Disappointment

Letdown is different from putdown; you react to each in a
different way.

A putdown is always inflicted by another. It is often
unmerited and usually unfair. It invites the worst within you
to strike back with a flattening putdown of the one who
tried first to flatten you.

Your letdowns, on the other hand, are often self-inflicted
wounds. Sure, someone you were counting on can fail to
deliver. That happens and it can leave you disappointed. But
typically it is you who puts an expectation out and up there as
preamble to what we politely call "a disappointment." Your
appointment with success may have been made hastily or
unrealistically; your dis-appointment—the broken appointment

with a hope, a dream, a desired and expected outcome—is of your own making. Realistic expectations are preventive medicine to protect against disappointment.

Beware of the tyranny of the promises you make to yourself. They can raise the bar too high. They can set too swift a pace. It is you telling you that you have to run that fast, jump that high. Who said so? You did. And in doing so, you set yourself up for disappointment.

Oliver Goldsmith may have seen you coming when he wrote: "As for disappointing them, I should not so much mind; but I can't abide to disappoint myself" (She Stoops to Conquer). You simply have to learn to abide your disappointments as part of the baggage you will lug through life. You'll do that more easily if you first become less concerned about disappointing "them," and more perceptive in noticing how your heightened expectations have a way of setting you up for an expectations crash.

Alexander Pope came up with a ninth Beatitude that says, "Blessed is the man who expects nothing, for he shall never be disappointed." Zero expectation is hardly a blessed state, in my view. Just weight your expectations with an appropriate measure of reality and you will move in restricted airspace, suited to low-level flights of fancy, on your way to realized dreams.

Lord, you know disappointment, because you know me.
I know I disappoint you at times; for that I ask
forgiveness.
I know disappointment too, often because I set my sights
too high.

Sometimes disappointment comes because I failed to
  prepare, or eased up a bit on the oar.
Either way, disappointment comes to me from time to time,
  and I need help.
Help me to keep my chin up.
Remind me to look ahead at the good things to come.
You promised never to break your appointment with me—
  your commitment, your covenant; why then should
  my broken appointments with you—my
  disappointments—ever get me down? Although I have
  disappointed you, you can never disappoint me.
  So why should minor disappointments turn me
  in on myself and away from you? You know the
  answer to that question, Lord, because you know me.
  All I can ask is that you save me from myself. Amen.

Sorrow

The very word conveys a notion of depth. The dimensions of sorrow run deep—inward and downward, straight to the soul.

"Sorry" is so often trivialized—"Oops! Sorry." "So sorry; could you repeat that?" Sorrow is anything but trivial. It cuts, wounds, pains, sinks your very being like a torpedo hitting its underwater target.

The causes of sorrow are as manifold as the secrets of the heart. Sorrow can be an invisible enemy or a clear and present danger fully framed and sharply focused in your consciousness. It can catch you unaware, or penetrate your awareness with a sting that just won't quit.

Sorrow's scalpel carves lines of sadness on faces that were meant to smile. "I'll never smile again" is a tolerable complaint in a love song, but incompatible with a faith-based life. How do you "snap out of it"? How do you break into a smile, face up to the future, and move on with trust into an unknown future?

Sorrow challenges you to paint your own sky blue, to keep the grass beneath your feet green, to block out the thunder and hear birds singing, to see calm seas behind the choppy waves. Sorrow can be managed. Ordinary people do it every day. They do it with the gift of faith.

Sorrow can prepare you to accept the gift of faith. For those who have faith in God and in themselves, sorrow can deepen their resolve to deal with unbelief, with the doubt that lies to you by saying, "this will never pass."

Some don't want it to pass because their sorrow is tied directly to the death of a loved one; they don't want the memory of that mourned and longed-for one to slip away. It won't. It will be there always in the vault of memory, available for recall. It will be present in the passing breeze, in morning sounds and evening stillness. But it can't be permitted to get in the way of forward progress in the march of life. Onward you go because you must; upward you look because you hope.

Sorrow encircles me from time to time, Lord.
I've been there in the depths.
I've walked hand in hand with a memory.
I know the pain.
I've lived long enough to see that sorrow touches every life,
*   and I can now bring myself to stop asking for*
*   exceptions to that rule.*

My sorrows can be turned to joy, I know, without
disrespecting a departed person whose absence
is the cause of the heaviness in my heart,
without ignoring the irreversible choices that may
have brought me low.
Work that miracle within me now, Lord, I pray; give me
resurrection joy.
Help me see the challenges the future puts before me;
let me heal the past and honor those no longer here
with deeds that extend their presence in our midst,
with love that reminds the world that you,
Lord, are still in charge!

Hope

Everything depends on hope. Everything. Without hope, there is little point in putting any hand to any plow; there is insufficient reason for facing any new day at any age or stage in life. Hopeless is as hopeless does: nothing, empty, zero.

I can't remember where I saw the cartoon cutline that had a workplace supervisor explaining to a visitor, "And the dim fluorescent lighting is intended to emphasize the absence of hope."

"Abandon hope all ye who enter here" is a posted warning to meet the eye of entrants to countless hells on earth in the world of work.

I'm puzzled at the way the word *hopefully* worked its misapplied way into our American vernacular. That adverb means "in a happily expectant way." Like "cheerfully," it conveys a mood. Hope is substance; hopefulness is style.

"Hopefully" suggests a bounce in your walk, some lilt in your voice.

Are you really "full of hope" and happily expectant when you say, "Hopefully"? Or are you not struggling with doubt and trying to sound brave? Instead of saying "hopefully," you should probably be saying—from the depths of doubt, discouragement, or perhaps even despair—"It is to be hoped" that this or that happy outcome will emerge. Go ahead, hope for it. Happy outcomes are indeed to be hoped for. Good results are possible.

Hope is an engine to drive your dreams into the unknown future.

It is wise to run an expectations check on yourself from time to time. Sure, the poet tells you that your reach should exceed your grasp "or what's a heaven for?" But too-long-a-reach can pull your arm out of its shoulder socket. Stretch but don't break. That goes for hopes as well as tendons.

We're talking moods in this chapter, and the mood of this particular moment is hopeful. Just as sorrow can make you sorrowful, hope can make you hopeful. From the inside, this mood feels good. From the outside, it is typically seen as something light, bright, and cheery, although it can work just as well under cover of seriousness. Hope is an anchor that connects you securely to God. The practice of hope can ground your being in God. And that's exactly where it ought to be!

Lord of all hopefulness,
Lord of all love.
My heart reaches out and up to you.

I'm not measuring; I'm just hoping.
I'm counting on you.
Life has its letdowns; that's not news to you, Lord, you've
heard it so often before from the likes of me.
But life has its lift-ups too, I've noticed.
And I'm counting on you to lift me up above my doubts
and disappointments, to help me lift myself up by
your good grace.
Hope, hope, and hope some more is my instruction to
myself.
Let me hear you say to me, Lord, that, hope by hope,
I'm making my way toward you.

Optimism

Raindrops may be falling on your head at any given moment, but you keep smiling. That smile is surely wide and may be close-lipped, but not at all smug.

It says hopeful.

It says yes.

Color it green not with envy, but with the brimming expectation that the best is yet to come. You know you don't have to be ill to get better, so you smile and wait for even better days ahead. That's optimism.

It is not a case of pasting a smile on your face to cover a furrowed brow. Nor is it a matter of using clowns' paint to transform sad features into wide-eyed cheerfulness. It is simply a condition of permitting the positive forces of life to shape your outlook, to give you the tilt, the "attitude," that points outward and upward toward the stars.

Sad that the infectious optimism of a child in the century-old novel *Pollyanna* has come to mean groundless good feeling in the face of harsh reality. There is neither virtue nor wisdom in acting "Pollyannaish."

The optimism that you should bring to prayer as well as to your down-to-earth dealings with other people should be reality-based. When the reality in your life is, by any fair measure, bad, your optimism points to a higher power, a greater love, another life called heaven, and an existence beyond all present imagining. Your optimism also assures you that you are going to have a good day tomorrow.

This is not something to be forced on others when you recognize that they just don't "get it." Nor is it something that you win through efforts of your own. It is gift. It is like the experience of being loved unconditionally. Just be your optimistic self and recognize—with gratitude—that you are privileged in your optimism to give others a glimpse of what God is like.

Here I am. Lord, optimistic and wondering why.
Wondering will neither add nor subtract from
my optimism; it will simply let me savor this good
feeling with a sense of deep-down gratitude.
I'm looking forward to tomorrow without looking away
from today.
The future is my friend, not a threat.
What lies ahead may be unknown but in moving toward it
I see myself stepping from one welcome mat to another on
my way to you.
Optimism lets me live comfortably in the present,
not complacently, but comfortably.

That comfort is a gift from you, a sign to me of
your presence.
I know that you are approached in prayer as
"Comforter of the Afflicted."
I also know that a realistic and not irreverent approach
sometimes sees you as the
"Afflicter of the Comfortable."
So don't let me grow overconfident or complacent, Lord;
just comfortably alert.
Keep me optimistic about my chances of never being
parted from you.

Pessimism

At the beginning of this chapter, I suggested that melancholy was a reasonable point of departure for a review of your moods. Melancholy is not quite the same thing as pessimism, although they are not unrelated.

Yogi Berra, the colorful New York Yankee catcher and manager, was famous for his malapropisms. He has a baseball-player son named Dale whose playing career was less distinguished, but his way with words certifies him as his father's son. When asked about what Yogi and he had in common, Dale replied: "Our similarities are completely different."

Melancholy and pessimism are similar but different. Borrowing from the poet John Dyer at the opening of this chapter, I noted, "there is a kindly mood of melancholy that wings the soul and points her to the skies." Pessimism points in the other direction. It clips the wings and fixes eyes downward. The pessimist moves through life on a blue route, seeing potential crashes at every intersection and viewing new opportunity as a failure waiting to happen. Change will inevitably make things worse. Sufficient for tomorrow is the grief that will surely be carried over from today. If you think things are bad now, just wait.

The pessimist has a tendency to underestimate everything and lives with the certainty of never being disappointed. Is it any wonder that pessimism and popularity have no more than an alphabetical affinity? Pessimists pollute the social environment and hang the crepe over any gathering of three or more. Unlike the melancholy person who wants to withdraw and can easily be lost in a crowd of three, the pessimist pumps dark clouds overhead, sees nothing but quicksand underfoot, yet noisily insists on leading the parade into the land of gloom.

And yet, and yet....There is something of the pessimist in us all.

I've often thought how fear of failure holds us back, keeps our sights too low, and makes pessimists of us all. Nothing surprising in the fact that you have met failure in the past and are likely to meet it again in the future. That's life. But so is goodness, ubiquitous goodness that shores up optimistic people out there. Sheer goodness can pick up the pessimists if they are open enough to accept it—open of eye to see it, open of heart to receive it. There is more than enough goodness to go around. It's a renewable resource. You can produce some yourself just by seeing good in others and letting the good within you move out to others.

Pessimism must never be permitted to become a state of mind, an occupying force. You can lead the revolution to overthrow that state. Just start seeing the good in yourself and others; try your hand at passing it around.

Color me blue in my pessimistic moments,
    Lord, and let me notice that skin tone
    right away.
Too often I've let pessimism pull me down and neglected
    to see how that mood can exercise a downward pull
    on others.
I guess that's another manifestation of the selfishness
    that I've just lately begun to recognize.
Lead me out of the blue and into your Green Pastures,
    Lord, not that I'm anxious for the afterlife,
    just looking for the green of hopeful optimism.
Better perhaps if I had the courage to pray that you shake
    me out of the blue, turn my eye outward toward
    others; my hands may start moving in that direction.
If that happens, I'll break out of the blue, I know.
It has happened before.
Whenever I turn my thoughts toward easing the burdens of
    others,
I find my own load lighter.
So help me to lighten up, Lord.
I know I'm safe in your keeping.
I just have to wonder why I let the pull of pessimism
    get me down.

Delight

Interesting, isn't it, to note how often "absolutely" is coupled with "delighted" when someone is really pleased? I am *absolutely delighted* that you have this book in your hands! I am really pleased.

Also interesting is the way (unknown to me) that the word *please,* which is related etymologically both to *pleasure* and to *plea,* worked itself into the way we give words to expressions of approval. I am pleased. I'm so pleased that I can say I'm delighted—absolutely delighted. What a pleasure!

The "light" in "delight" points to the meaning of the word that colors your mood in reaction to pleasurable surprise. It is a mood you've often known, enjoyed, and want to keep. It brightens your life, illumines your memory, enlightens your mind, and throws light over the path ahead enabling you to move forward.

Delight helps you pick up your pace and move with confidence into the future. But delight can exit your experience abruptly; it can depart for other climes or shores, leaving you stranded. A strand, as you know, is a shoreline. The once delighted you, can find yourself playing the lead role in your personal sequel to the Tom Hanks "survivor" movie. When delight departs, you can be set adrift; you can find yourself stranded. When delight departs, darkness moves in. Could it be that the letter "n" serves to negate and replace the "l" in "light" and signals that you have been driven into "night," into darkness? Loneliness and panic can ensue.

Spiritual or religious experience is no stranger to delight. Tradition encourages you to "delight in the Lord." Spirituality knows the "dark night of the soul," but the Lord's delight in you and your delight to be in the presence of the Lord are more dominant themes in the faith experience of those who trust and are willing to place themselves in the hands of God.

Some people take delight in poetry; others delight in dessert. The "Garden of Earthly Delights" may or may not be familiar to you. What is it, or who is it that really delights you? The deeper the delight, the more substantial the cause is likely to be. The farther removed it is from dependency on your credit card, the more likely the source of your delight is something really substantial and likely to last.

People lie all the time about being "delighted" to meet strangers they may well never see again. Not that the meeting is unpleasant; it just doesn't mean much. To be genuinely delighted in and with the presence of another person is a gift to be treasured. When delight dominates your mood, shapes your outlook, and puts a smile on your face, you are ready to turn that face toward God.

Lord, I'm delighted to be in your presence.
It calms me, just to know that you are near.
There is a lot about myself that is not all that delightful,
*   to my eye at least; that's why it is hard for me,*
*   frankly, to delight in your presence, even though*
*   I want to be there.*
Knowing you is my delight, and yet I know you only dimly
*   and darkly.*
Loving you is my delight, and yet my love gives
*   way to fear.*
Following your will is, I know, the route to happiness and
*   eternal delight, yet detours keep looking good and*
*   take me where I really should not go.*

Then delight slips away, leaving me stranded, not defeated,
*   just adrift with nothing to delight me but myself,*
*   and how well I've come to know the emptiness*
*   of all that.*
So delight me once again, Lord, with your presence,
*   with your grace, and with the knowledge*
*   of your love for me.*

Gratitude

I've said it often and would argue the point anytime, that if I were pressed to reduce the entire meaning of religion to one word, that word would be gratitude. The case for making that one word *love* instead of *gratitude* is worth attempting, but I recall learning that it was God who first loved us, thus enabling us to love—by his good gift of love—and therefore all we can be is grateful. Why? Because he first loved us; he graced us.

I am also fond of reminding anyone who cares to listen that the old American vernacular used to express gratitude by simply saying, "much obliged." Obligation under God springs from a sense of gratitude. Think about that. Acknowledge gratitude as your only stance before God, and you begin to notice the presence of moral obligation to do or not do certain things that God wants you to do or avoid.

Chesterton had something profound in mind when he wrote "thanks are the highest form of thought; and... gratitude is happiness doubled by wonder." I'm not sure what he meant by that, but it sounds good to me!

There is a multiplier effect associated with gratitude, and the wonder of it all is that gratitude can, if you let it stretch your mind, magnify your happiness.

I once knew a small-time politician who was constantly being bothered by people looking for jobs in city government. "Six people want the job," he told me. "You get it for one and wind up with one ingrate and five enemies." Success and security can make ingrates of us all. That's more than a bit strange, but nonetheless true. Perhaps it is saying something about self and selfishness, or it may simply be spelling out a little lesson in human nature, which does have an insular, self-enclosing, self-interested tendency. Perhaps that relates to the survival instinct. But human nature is also social, relational, outward reaching, needing to link and bond. But will human nature share—naturally? Not easily and perhaps not naturally, but it would be simply erroneous to contend that sharing is unnatural when human happiness depends on it. So we have to learn to share. And we learn through various stages of growth and the development of our sense of gratitude.

What stage of growth are you in now? The closer you get to open and generous sharing, the clearer the signal you are sending to others that gratitude is driving your decisions.

There are stages in your moral development too, in your degree of growth in gratitude, in showing yourself to be "much obliged." Where are you now? The higher you rise above a childish "avoid-getting-caught" morality to a principled "doing-the-right-thing" stage—doing it regardless of who notices and of any reward except knowing that you did the right thing—the more refined your sense of gratitude is.

In any case, gratitude is the ground of moral obligation, and being grateful is the best way of declaring your dependency on God. Count your blessings and be thankful.

I could start counting now, Lord,
*   and I would be at it for days taking inventory*
*   of your blessings to me.*
Forgive me for not noticing them more readily
*   and more often.*
When everything is going well, I rarely think of pausing to
*   say thanks.*
That's simply wrong of me and terribly immature.
Now that I am taking a moment to think about it,
I'm beginning to notice the arrogance in my refusal to say
*   thanks and the selfishness of putting myself on center*
*   stage without a nod to playwright, producer,*
*   and supporting cast, not to mention the folks who*
*   built the theater and sold the tickets.*
Let me shun for this brief moment the spotlight I crave
*   in order to find the humility I need.*
And there, on the ruins of my self-centeredness,
I pray for an abiding sense of gratitude. One word turns
*   my heart to you: gratias!*

Wonder

The "wonder of it all," we often remark to ourselves in the face of beauty and power. "All lost in wonder" is the poet Gerard Manley Hopkins's description of himself in the presence of God.

"I wonder about that," says the doubter who is, in fact, certain of a contrary opinion. "I wonder" is a verbal visa providing entry into neutral territory in the world of argument.

"Wonderful" is an overworked word in our era of underdeveloped vocabularies. And "wondering" is a form of mental wandering from idea to idea, observation to observation, as the one who wonders tries to connect the dots that reality scatters before the mind's eye. Yes, the wonder of it all!

In human experience, wondering is like ventilation. It is not just like the air; it is the air of the imagination. The mind breathes it in and breathes it out. You wonder. And if you were ever to stop wondering, others would begin to wonder whether you were still there!

Think for a moment now about what you typically label "wonderful." Make a mental list of the things you tend to "wonder about." Your "wonderings" may be banal or profound. Typically, if you follow the trail of your "wonderings," you will find yourself moving into the depths of yourself, your world, and your God.

How flat existence would be in the absence of all wonder. How rich life is when enhanced by wonder. So run a wonder inventory at this moment in your life. Perhaps a wonder history would be helpful; it could lead to recovery of forgotten wonders and retrieval of mental keepsakes that are capable of reigniting wonder in your life right now.

We carry within us the wonders we long to enjoy. A prayer interval at any time in a busy day, can, God willing, let a sense of wonder surface in our awareness and work its magic in our hearts.

Wonderful.
Am I full of wonder? Not now, Lord.
Not me. Not me, at least, not yet!
I'm full of hope, and hopeful that a sense of wonder will
*   touch me from time to time.*
It has in the past. It will again, I know.
And when it does, it always brings me closer to you, Lord.
What a wonderful world!
I hear those words in song and want to shout, "amen!"
I walk those words in early morning, or at sunset, and with
them speak your praise.
You are great; I am grateful.
If I were holier, I, too, could become "all lost in wonder."
I'm not there yet.
I'm not lost, just moving along in the right direction.
And wonder is within my reach—
*   wonder in the presence of a newborn child;*
*   wonder at the prairies, plains, mountains, valleys,*
*   seas and shores;*
*   wonder at the kindnesses I see;*
*   wonder at the talent I notice in others and sometimes*
*   in myself;*
*   wonder at the reflections of your wisdom and*
*   goodness reflected in all that causes me to wonder.*

Confusion

"I'm confused" is a genuine common-denominator expression. Who do you know who has never uttered those words? It is a "been-there, done-that" dimension of everyone's existence. You've been confused. Perhaps you are now confused. You will surely be confused at some point in the not-too-distant future. (I may even manage to confuse you within the confines of this short reflection!)

"Don't confuse me with the facts," you've heard others say many times. That's usually meant to be a dismissive quip, but it is sometimes true that facts can indeed be confusing. You can become confused just trying to understand facts that are not easily grasped. A multiplicity of facts, although all comprehensible and each understood, can also confuse the mind, which, you've noticed long ago, is made for unity. A unifying theme can make multiple facts manageable to the mind.

When you are confused, try to extricate yourself from that swamp by articulating a unifying theme. Repeat the theme. Take it as a marching order. Follow it through the confusion on out to a state of mind where all is clear (or just a bit clearer) once again.

The unifying theme may be a simple principle that you've internalized and prize highly. Think of how you have already articulated (at least to yourself) principles of justice, fairness, compassion, forgiveness, competition, or restitution. Recall the moral principles that you tend to apply to your choices in the areas of money, property, health, sexuality, politics, faith, and family relations. And when your "I'm confused" complaint emerges from or centers on any one of these areas, think of the conviction, the principle you've internalized, that can function as a unifying theme. This is another way of saying: Let your conscience be your guide. Your conscience is formed by principled convictions.

If, for example, you think "living generously in the service of others" is a key to happiness, apply that conviction as a sorter when you are confused by competing claims on your time and talent. If, for another example, you understand sexuality as having much to do with the service of life, use that conviction to guide you through the push and pull of emotion and passion associated with your awareness of your own sexuality. To offer another example, if your confusion is produced by a series of doubts, remind yourself that faith is the condition of entrusting yourself to God, and simply trust. Like a passing cloud, confusion will lift.

Every once in awhile, you have to take a Saturday off and apply yourself to cleaning up the mess, straightening things up, attending to the unattended chaos in the place where you live. There's a parallel there to how you should deal with the confusion that accumulates between your ears. Sit down and sort it out. Don't cling to unmade choices that keep you in the undecided column. Just as you throw things out in your Saturday morning cleanup, cut through the clutter of pending possibilities and make your personal declaration of independence from unnecessary confusion. On that firm note, you may want to pause to pray:

Let your light lift my confusion, Lord,
the way the rising sun burns off the morning fog.
Sometimes it's up to me, I know, to do some lifting,
and I'll try.
But only in you will I find my way toward clarity.

Confusion need not paralyze me, unless I want that
      to happen.
I want not to be rash, imprudent, or abrupt, but I would
      like to be decisive.
Teach me the relationship between incision and decision;
      give me the courage to decide in a way that cuts
      through the confusion.
When several conflicting mental forces fuse within my
      mind, I'm confused.
When your light breaks through,
      the forces separate so that
      I can handle them one by one, toward clarity,
      toward peace, toward a reassuring amen.

Fear

Fear is part of the coin you need to pay your dues for membership in the human race. No one can go through life without the experience of fear.

Fear makes the positive contribution of defending (or at least warning) you against danger. In the ordinary, everyday, common-sense meaning of the word, fear can weigh you down, knock you out, hold you back, destroy your peace of mind, force you to withdraw, and rob your heart of happiness. The Christian tradition reminds those who are faithful, but also fearful, that love can drive out fear. Keep that in mind as you think about fear in your life.

A not so ordinary and far less obvious understanding of the word would equate fear with reverence. "Fear of the Lord," a familiar expression in several religious traditions, should be understood in this way. Your reverence before the

Lord is an expression of fear of the Lord. This is not servile fear, and most assuredly not neurotic fear. It is reverence and awe in the face of an awe-inspiring reality, namely, the presence of an all-knowing, all-powerful, all-loving God in your life.

What a distortion of this special meaning of fear when someone threatens to "put the fear of God in you!" God is never to be feared in a display of fright-filled cowering. You show your fear of God in reverence. Fear your own capacity to reject your God, but have no fear that God will ever reject you.

"Fearless" is a quality often attributed to persons who do heroic things. Sometimes those who seem to be fearless are insufficiently aware (perhaps too dumb to comprehend) the real danger in a given situation. When all the hazards are noted and fully understood, the one who is "fearless" is one who has overcome fear, not one who is without fear.

Most of us have to learn how to manage our fears as we move forward, rather than permitting fear to hold us back. A rabbit's foot is no guarantee of safe passage. Putting your own foot forward, despite the fears that seem to be closing in on you, is the only way to go.

Of what are you afraid? What fears weigh you down? Make mental notes or jot them down on paper. You'll sort them out in general categories like health, money, and work, or in more personal folders that catalogue your phobias. That will be like looking at yourself in a house of mirrors. Be fair enough to yourself to acknowledge that the images those mirrors throw back are distorted. You can work out the distortions with professional help, if you need it, or by just laughing at yourself (as everyone does in a house of mirrors) and moving on.

It's been said that anyone who harbors any kind of fear is "landlord to a ghost." The point is worth considering. Some of your fears point to the past, but the past is dead (it's a ghost). Some point to the future, but the future may never arrive, at least not in the form that you now anticipate (that ghost may never show up). Why permit an invisible enemy like fear to pull you out of the present moment, the only moment that is fully in your possession?

Most of that which you fear does not exist, at least does not exist in the present moment, the only place where you live. You have to remember that a life lived in fear is a life half-lived, so handing yourself over to present fears means giving up a valuable portion of your life. Handing yourself over to fears of the past puts you in the custody of a ghost. And turning yourself over to fears about the future "gives up the ghost," as they say, leaving you helpless and, go ahead and say it, afraid. It makes no sense.

You can make a lot of sense by taking charge of your life, which is another way of saying, taking charge of your fears. If you have trouble doing that, get professional help. If you can do it with difficulty, get to work right now because it will not be easier at any time in the future.

Take a minute now to pray your fears down to manageable size.

Fear of failure.
Fear of the dark.
Fear of illness.
Fear of rejection.
Fear of discovery.
Fear of speaking up, or out, or saying it in public.
Fear of losing my job.
Fear of harm to those I love.
Fear of hating those who do me harm.
Fear of heights, of depths, of water, and of fire.
Fear of falling.
Fear of abandonment, engulfment, annihilation.
Fear of those who want (I think) to do me harm.
Why should I be afraid of all these, Lord,
  and of so much more?
It can only be because I think I'm altogether on my own,
  away from you, out of touch, and out of reach.
The power is yours, Lord; certain tasks are mine.
I'll do what I can; I'll muddle through somehow,
  because I believe that you are here and I have
  nothing to fear.
Nothing.
Amen.

Terror

We tend to use mood words loosely. Disaster, for example. The cake may collapse in the oven, but that is hardly a disaster. Similarly, your failure to reassemble all the parts of your malfunctioning timepiece cannot claim a place on any list of genuine disasters.

    It is often the same with terror. "I was terrified" adds to the zest of your first-person account of a dangerous situation, but the fact that you were able to work yourself out of it suggests that you were not, in fact, terrorized. Terror carries a freezing, incapacitating connotation. There is also something sudden about it. Terror tends to take you by surprise. Moreover, terror seldom comes in small doses. I was "filled" with terror, not half or three-quarters, but "filled," say those who live to talk about it.

And how about feeling "terrible" or "terrific"—what about their link to terror? Terrific is, in the vocabulary of mood swings, the opposite of terrible, and yet that "terr," "terr," "terr" is there to cut you—up or down—to the quick. Terrific says exhilaration; terrible punctures your balloon, or worse. "He hath loosed the fateful lightning of his terrible swift sword."

Since September 11, 2001, the whole world has a heightened sense of terror, a better understanding of the mind of terrorists, and an almost fatalistic acceptance of terrorism as an any-day, everywhere possibility. What a way to have to live! Those who, despite terrorist acts, remain sound of both mind and body take prudent measure of the presence of terrorist threats, and the possibility of terrorist attacks, but refuse to permit terror to become their tutor regarding choices in the conduct of their lives. We all want and are willing to work for homeland security. We can indeed become more secure, but we realize that there is no ultimate and ever-reliable defense against malice. Terrorists can attack at any time. That does not, however, mean that we have to live in terror.

Faith is your shield against any possible assault. Even when your body is under attack, your soul cannot be harmed. Even when your mind is full of fear and at the breaking point, your spirit need not collapse. Faith, an immaterial, weightless, spiritual reality, is your protective shield. It is completely portable.

Neither terror nor terrorists can overcome faith, which is to say that faith can always overcome both terror and terrorism. You can choose to make it so.

I am the sum of my choices, Lord, and I choose you.
I choose you to be my refuge, my fortress, my defender.
Faith convinces me that you are always there for me;
*   experience has taught me that I cannot save myself.*
Without you, Lord, I am defenseless against terrifying
*   thoughts as well as terrorist attacks.*
Both have the potential to paralyze me.
Only you can cure that paralysis.
Help me to understand and to accept that in the absolutely
*   worst possible case—the destruction of both mind*
*   and body by terrorist attack—there cannot be any*
*   destruction of the part of me that will live forever.*
I take that on faith.
I put my faith in you, Lord.
And that's an irreversible choice I'm making now—
*   and forever. Amen.*

Anger

Everyone knows what anger is. They know it from personal experience. Some study the phenomenon and come to understand its psychological underpinnings and emotional dimensions. All should understand, but many refuse to accept the fact that anger, in just the right amount, is a normal, even healthy response to reality. The challenge, of course, is in keeping anger down to just the right amount. Out-of-control anger turns into rage. If anger moves outside the range of normal, it can be sinful and potentially destructive.

Anger can be with self. When driven deeply inward, anger can turn into depression.

When turned outward toward others, anger can lead to violence, even to destruction of property and persons (or to be more precise, of life, because the person whose life is lost will nevertheless live forever). Anger must, therefore, be managed, and one way of managing it is to accept it as a reminder that you are alive and well, but at risk of doing harm to yourself, or others, or both. Knowing that you are in harm's way, you become cautious. There's the key: caution.

In the old days, traffic engineers referred to the yellow or amber light between red and green on a traffic signal as the "caution light." Slow down; move cautiously and carefully.

When I was fifteen, not yet old enough to drive, I learned a lesson about safe driving at a blinking "caution" or amber light at the corner of School House Lane and Wissahickon Avenue in Philadelphia. The father of a friend was driving four of us boys home from a sports-awards dinner. As his car approached this intersection, a blinking yellow light advised caution. He slowed down to a virtual stop. I pointed out that cars that might come into the intersection from either left or right had a red blinker facing them and there was no need for us to stop. My friend's father explained that late at night, you never know if the other fellow is going to stop, so you better be cautious and slow down to a crawl. Lesson learned.

And so it is with anger. Be slow to anger. Let it blink you down to a slower speed. Out-of-control anger can be nothing but harmful to yourself and others. The fact of the matter is that anger can kill. The death-dealing potential of anger is the reason why moral boundaries have to be imposed on angry feelings. "Anger is a short madness," wrote Horace more than twenty centuries ago; by keeping your anger short you guarantee your safe return to sanity.

Sure, you can kick the dog or punch the wall and claim that it makes you "feel better," but all that does is move you a few notches closer to hurting yourself or someone you love. You can use those angry feelings as an excuse not to repair relationships at home or at work. You can substitute rage and revenge for your rightful participation in the human construction project that strengthens human community through applications of compassion and understanding.

No one's perfect. But neither is anyone exempt from the duty of holding him- or herself in hand when emotions rise to threaten the peace in human relationships. Not to do so is to encourage the assault of anger on all that is good, and decent, and capable of making you and your world more fully human.

I think I tend to take it too lightly, Lord, my anger, that is.
I tend not to see any danger in losing my temper,
cursing my bad luck, speaking sharply to anyone
within earshot, being just plain pugnacious.

Irritability is something I think I can live with and
    manage to control.
But even there I make dumb choices about rest, nutrition,
    and related matters that,
if unattended, will make me irritable.
The more damaging choice, I know, is to let the irritability
    ignite a meanness streak that can hurt others
    (while not doing me any good either!).
The bigger problem, I realize, goes way beyond irritability.
It is the angry response to real or imagined wrongs,
    the lashing out when I feel threatened,
    the scorn I show, the contempt I deliver, the ridicule
    I heap on others whose human dignity I not simply
    ignore but choose to walk all over.
Do pride and anger go together, Lord? They have to if my
    experience is any guide.
Arrogance is offspring of my pride, and arrogance is
    anger's breeding ground.
So all of this brings me to prayer.
I pray for wisdom, for humility, for the grace to hold
    myself in check, and to be sorry for the times
    I've turned my better self over to the thief called anger
    that knows how to break into my house
    and take away my humanity bit by bit.
I want, with your help, Lord, to catch that thief right now.
    Amen.

Rage

Simply saying the word moves you forward in your chair.
The sound of the word elevates your shoulders and tightens
your fingers into two fists ready for action. "Raging bull"
and "road rage" are likely to pop up on your mental screen

these days. "It's the rage!" may have an echo chamber some-where in your memory, but that expression points in another more pleasant direction.

We're not talking "rant and rave." This is high voltage, two-hundred horsepower "rage" that's on the table, my reader friend, for your reflection at the moment.

The word finds its way into the world of rock music and video games. There's a lot of bang and crash associated with seeing or hearing rage in pop culture. Like smoking, violence has never done anyone any good. Once you realize that, however, you are faced with the challenge of breaking the addiction.

First, you have to notice its presence; you have to look for traces of rage in your life and then begin to deal with them.

Shakespeare finds a remedy for rage in music. One who is "full of rage," writes the Bard, will find that music can "change his nature." "The man that hath no music in him-self./ Nor is not moved with concord of sweet sounds,/ Is fit for treasons, stratagems, and spoils./ The motions of his spirit are dull as night,/ And his affections dark as Erebus [Hell]/ Let no such man be trusted. Mark the music" (Lorenzo to Jessica in *The Merchant of Venice*, Act V, Scene 1).

So "mark the music" in your own life and notice the "motions" of your spirit as you not simply mark, but march to the music of your moods. Rage breaks into a run rather than moving apace. It breaks into a roar instead of speaking simply. It is brutish rather than bold, demanding and not easily tamed. But tame it you must if you want to retain your human dignity and respect the dignity of others. Uncontrolled rage can make animals of us all.

I find myself saying from time to time, Lord,
　　"I'm outraged."
And to be truthful, I have to admit to the presence of some
　　self-righteousness when I do.
I elevate myself to a level of indignation
　　and condemn what I see below as bad, reprehensible,
　　"outrageous."
I can't help wondering why I see rage within me as bad
　　and outrage as good, even virtuous.
Does rage somehow change its stripes when it gets "out"?
But this is not the time to play with words.
I need to pray for control.
Be with me, Lord, when the boiling point approaches.
Dampen down my anger before it stretches into rage.
Help me to see myself as insecure whenever
　　I'm tempted to "rant and rage,"
　　(whatever ranting means as preamble to rage!).
I'm capable of losing control, but that won't happen if I
　　don't first lose you, Lord.
So hold me tight and hold me down.
This won't destroy me, I know;
your loving hold will
　　simply prevent me from destroying myself
　　through rage.
With thanks, therefore, I say: amen.

Shame

In recent years, I've become convinced that there just is not enough shame in the world. Whether they are shedding spouses in order to "find themselves," or shedding clothing with an eye to titillation and sexual attraction, otherwise "respectable" people either do or gleefully observe others doing outrageous (there I go again!) things.

Language that would make a sailor blush is heard in the corridors of middle schools. Ethical standards that hoodlums would regard as embarrassingly low pass as guidelines for right conduct in many corners of the American business system. Shred the documents. Bend the truth. Pocket the profits. Greed is good.

I want to be me; and me, of course, is always first.

Human dignity—what's that? We live in something of a throwaway society (successor perhaps to the affluent society) and we now notice that people, even children, are being thrown away along with all our other trash. Have we no shame?

A tracer can be put on the trail of disappearing shame in contemporary society by looking for it through the lens of embarrassment. Shortly after getting it straight that the word has two "s's" and two "r's," young people have relatively little use for "embarrassment" in their vocabularies. Nothing seems to embarrass them.

Evidence of the disappearance of embarrassment ranges over a wide field marked off by late arrivals for appointments (no apology), no thank-you notes (who says you have to do that?), fake IDs (drinking laws are silly), binge drinking (it eases stress), premarital sex (it feels good), cohabitation (everybody's doing it), abortion (I'm not ready for a child), drug abuse (I'm bored), theft (I'm only doing it to get by), infidelity (I'm weak), and on and on it goes through all age cohorts and class differences. It is not the wrong conduct or moral lapses that are remarkable; it is the willingness to be publicly identified with the conduct that prompts one to ask: What ever became of shame?

Shame is linked with humiliation in human experience. It is an affect, a feeling. Shame is subject to rational control, and it can be reasoned away as one comes to understand that this feeling of humiliation has no right to permanent residency in one's life. It can also be "rationalized" away in the sense of convincing oneself that there is no basis at all for feeling ashamed. The rationalization machine can bend the mind into thinking that just about any vice is in fact a virtue, something of which to be proud! Or, one can simply become desensitized to that which should and will, in normal circumstances, cause a person to feel shame—to be ashamed. The feeling is there for a purpose. Like fear, shame has a warning function; it exercises a protective role.

If society wants to protect its members, old and young, from the consequences of drug and alcohol abuse, theft and fraud, sexual promiscuity and related misconduct, from hurtful behavior of any kind, it must find ways to bring back shame, to reintroduce the shield of shame in human affairs. This means being willing, as a society, to take a stand, to draw some lines. As the old saying goes, if you don't stand for something, you'll fall for anything. That seems to be happening more and more in our day. It is reflected in diminishing and disappearing standards of good taste in entertainment, of fairness in business, and of professional integrity (including, sad to say, professionals in the ranks of clergy, who are supposed to be setting the standards).

What you do in secret is a disclosure of your character. Shame can serve to tutor and strengthen character so that what one would not, because of good character, do in secret, will not be done in public. Shame can serve all of us well.

There are times when I'm ashamed of myself, Lord,
*   you know that, and I don't intend to get into any of*
*   the reasons for it here.*
It is enough for me to know that you know not only that I
*   am capable of doing shameful things, but also capable*
*   of feeling ashamed,*
*   and that, for me, Lord, is reassuring.*
I thank you for the gift of shame.
I hope I can use it to reduce my propensity to do
*   shameful deeds!*
Help me, and the world in which I live, to bring back
*   shame, Lord.*
It is your world. It is being harmed, which is to say your
*   people are being harmed, by the absence of shame.*
*   The gates are open to all kinds of harmful excesses.*
The shield of shame can protect us, Lord.
Help us to have the wisdom and courage to bring it back.
We all know we become better persons when we bring
*   ourselves to say, "I'm sorry."*
Teach us how to become better persons by seeing
*   the wisdom of saying, "I'm ashamed."*

Guilt

It is my experience that, even in our rather permissive society, most people are too hard on themselves. The reason for this, I think, is guilt. For some strange reason, we find it difficult to accept forgiveness, or, to put it another way, we find it difficult to accept ourselves as forgiven. We cannot securely and confidently turn the page, start anew, and move ahead believing that all is well between ourselves and God.

You, my reader friend, are the resident expert on your own guilt. I'm not an analyst or therapist; nor are you a patient on this page. You're just like so many other good people who feel the need to pause for prayer, but once you slow down, it sometimes happens that you become aware of a troubling little tug of guilt that makes you uneasy and, in fact, blocks your path to God. Be sure you know the difference between being guilty and being driven by guilt.

There are, of course, some who clearly have a lot to feel guilty about, and they know it beyond the shadow of doubt. A forgiving God can extricate them from their moral guilt, if they entrust themselves to God's mercy. Freedom from their emotional guilt is another matter. That puddle might just not dry up; that candle may not all that easily go out.

Facing God in prayer sometimes requires courage—not presumption or arrogance, just courage. See God's forgiveness and accept the fact that you have been forgiven. Facing up to your friends (or anyone else, for that matter) when you know you are guilty of offending them takes courage too. You must first face up to yourself and then present yourself in person or in writing to the one whom you've hurt, and ask forgiveness. Then you can acknowledge that you have done what is required of you, so stop feeling guilty and get on with your life.

But, no, it's still there. You still feel guilty. Manage that guilt carefully. Get professional help if you need it. But you can first try managing it out of your way. Be as reasonable with yourself as you would be with your own child or a good friend. Reassure yourself. You've done your best; rely on God to take care of the rest. Let go of your guilt.

Lord, if it were only that easy.
If only I could say goodbye to guilt and watch it go
away—forever.
But it just doesn't work that way.
I keep pointing the finger at myself.
I refuse to let myself off the hook.
I have to wonder whether I'm getting some strange satis-
faction from feeling guilty.
Is that what "wallowing" means? Am I just wallowing
in my guilt?
Bring me to my senses, Lord.
Come to think of it, that's where most of my guilt resides,
in the senses.
I feel guilty, so I need you to let me say so long to guilt,
to start feeling otherwise, to start feeling free,
to stop feeling guilty.
You can do it, Lord.
And with your help, so can I.

It's been said that people in a hurry cannot feel. I have to wonder about that. I suspect that feelings often fuel the haste. Slowing down is good for the soul. Whatever mood you find yourself in, my reader friend, slow down and rest away a few prayerful moments with the Lord. Let these pages be your guide to those prayerful moments. And don't for a moment question your qualifications to fashion prayers of your own.

Your moods will, as I've already indicated, shift. Let yourself slip away now from any preoccupation you might have with yourself, and how your feel, and all the rest of what goes along with being "in touch" with yourself. Just be yourself and be comfortable with thanking God that you are who and what you are.

And remember always to pray for others. That's what a sequel to this book, available in a year or so, will encourage you to do. Meanwhile, work your way in and out of the prayers between the covers of this book. Think of them as fifty-five originals paving the way for your homemade, heartfelt expressions of reverence, awe, and wonder in the presence of a God who loves you more than you could ever imagine.

Afterword

Prayer and Desire

Augustine of Hippo (354–430) who, as everyone knows, made a monumental contribution to the shaping of Western thought, had many interesting things to say about prayer. I end this book with the following quotation from St. Augustine's Letter to Proba. His thoughts will, I hope, help the reader continue to think about enlarging both the desire for God in prayer and the capacity to receive from God the good things that are held in store by God for those who ask for them in prayer. These are words to be read slowly and aloud—to yourself in a quiet setting, to others in a faith sharing environment. Don't rush. Just listen to Augustine.

Why in our fear of not praying as we should, do we turn to so many things, to find what we should pray for? Why do we not say instead, in the words of the psalmist: "I have asked one thing from the Lord, this is what I will seek: to dwell in the Lord's house all the days of my life, to see the graciousness of the Lord, and to visit his temple." There, the days do not come and go in succession, and the beginning of one day does not mean the end of another; all days are one, simultaneously and without end, and the life lived out in these days has itself no end.

So that we might obtain this life of happiness, he who is true life itself taught us to pray, not in many words as though speaking longer could gain us a hearing. After all, we pray to one who, as the Lord himself tells us, knows what we need before we ask for it.

Why he should ask us to pray, when he knows what we need before we ask him, may perplex us if we do not realize that our Lord and God does not want to know what we want (for he cannot fail to know it) but wants us rather to exercise our desire through our prayers, so that we might be able to receive what he is preparing to give us. His gift is very great indeed, but our capacity is too small and limited to receive it. That is why we are told "Enlarge your desires, do not bear the yoke with unbelievers."

The deeper our faith, the stronger our hope, the greater our desire, the larger will be our capacity to receive that gift, which is very great indeed. "No eye has seen it"; it has no color. "No ear has heard it"; it has no sound. "It has not entered man's heart"; man's heart must enter into it.

In this faith, hope, and love, we pray always with unwearied desire. However, at set times and seasons we also pray to God in words, so that by these signs we may instruct ourselves and mark the progress we have made in our desire, and spur ourselves on to deepen it. The more fervent the desire, the more worthy will be its fruit. When the Apostle [Paul] tells us, "Pray without ceasing," he means this: Desire unceasingly that life of happiness which is nothing if not eternal, and ask it of him who alone is able to give it.

Acknowledgments

The idea for this book originated with my agent, Michael Snell, whose suggestions and encouragement I much appreciate. I am also grateful to my Jesuit friend Father Jerry Campbell, former director of the Center for Ignatian Spirituality at Holy Trinity Catholic Church in Washington, DC, who read the manuscript and provided helpful comments.

I was serving as pastor at Holy Trinity when the events of September 11, 2001, occurred. Prayer and conversations with Holy Trinity parishioners in the months after that fateful day helped to shape many of the thoughts that have found their way onto these pages. Simple justice requires that I thank them; ordinary prudence prompts me to absolve them from any responsibility for the published outcome of our shared reflections.

Also by William J. Byron, SJ
from other publishers

Toward Stewardship (1975)

The Causes of World Hunger (editor, 1982)

Quadrangle Considerations (1989)

Take Courage: Psalms of Support and Encouragement
(editor, 1995)

Finding Work without Losing Heart (1995)

Answers from Within (1998)

Jesuit Saturdays (2000)